DESIGNER TEXTILES

STITCHING FOR INTERIORS

DESIGNER TEXTILES
STITCHING FOR INTERIORS

THE EMBROIDERERS' GUILD

PHOTOGRAPHS BY DUDLEY MOSS
TEXT BY FIONA ADAMCZEWSKI

A DAVID & CHARLES CRAFT BOOK

British Library Cataloguing in Publication Data

Adamczewski, Fiona
   Designer textiles : stitching for
   interiors.
   1. Embroidery – Great Britain
   I. Title   II. Moss, Dudley
   III. Embroiderers' Guild
   746.44'0941   NK9243

   ISBN 0-7153-9040-6

Printed in The Netherlands
by Smeets Offset BV, Weert
for David & Charles Publishers plc
Brunel House   Newton Abbot   Devon

Distributed in the United States by
Sterling Publishing Co., Inc., 2 Park Avenue,
New York, NY 10016

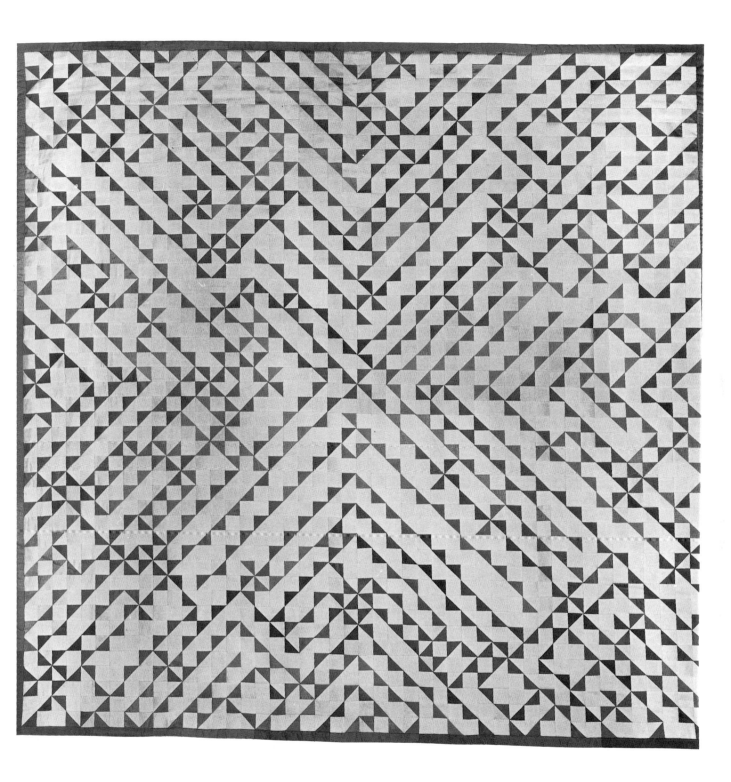

Contents

INTRODUCTION

How do embroidery artists work? Where does their inspiration come from. What techniques do they use to achieve the desired colours, textures and overall effect? Embroidery has changed so radically in recent years that the answers to these questions are not immediately apparent when looking at a stitched picture or hanging.

Designer Textiles aims to capture the excitement of modern embroidery and to demonstrate how leading exponents of the craft set about their work. It is based on the exhibits in the first-ever exhibition by Britain's leading embroidery artists.

'Stitched Textiles for Interiors', organised by the Embroiderers' Guild at the Royal Institute of British Architects in 1986, aimed to show the excellence of modern embroidery and, in particular, to encourage architects and interior designers to place commissions.

The exhibition was a great success. It attracted over 450 visitors each day. A good percentage of the exhibits sold and commissions have since been placed with exhibitors. The standard of work was extremely high. The great variety of designs, textures, techniques, and colours ranging from minimal pastels to brilliant hues surprised and delighted those who had not seen embroidery for some years.

Each artist interprets a subject in their own way. A landscape by Kate Wells or Verina Warren looks tranquil and inviting whereas the dark rocks and swirling crows by Eirian Short are positively menacing. Buildings are treated quite differently by Beryl Dean, Esther Grainger and Jean Littlejohn, so too are the self portraits by Mary Cozens-Walker and Paddy Ramsay. For sheer stitchery you have to admire the work of Rosalind Floyd and Margaret Hall. Look too for the abstract work of Beverley Clark, Mary Spyrou, Ann Sutton and Katherine Virgils, and the paper superbly used by Sally Freshwater, Jean Davey Winter and Stephanie Tuckwell.

Enthusiastic embroiderers and City and Guilds students were at the exhibition with their note books and magnifying glasses, peering at details, sketching designs and making copious notes. This book will answer many of their questions and help them to solve their problems.

In Britain, embroidery has been used as an artistic medium since the late nineteenth century and is now taught as a degree subject in art colleges and polytechnics. Consequently we have the best embroidery artists in the world. Embroidery is, though, the Cinderella of the art world in that it receives far too little publicity. As the new Chairman of the Embroiderers' Guild I was in a position to try and rectify this by persuading the Guild to sponsor an exhibition showing the very best contemporary work.

Since its inception in 1906, the Guild has a distinguished record of organising exhibitions of both contemporary and historic embroidery. There have been regular exhibitions of selected members' work and, more recently, major exhibitions featuring different aspects of its magnificent Collection of historic embroideries have been shown in museums here and abroad.

'Stitched Textiles for Interiors' was a completely new departure in that it exhibited the work of an invited group of artists (regardless of whether they were members of the Guild) chosen by three very distinguished embroiderers: Constance Howard, MBE, ARCA; Audrey Walker, who succeeded her as head of textiles/fashion at Goldsmiths' College, University of London; and Anthea Godfrey, senior lecturer, department of design, at The London College of Fashion.

The exhibition was organised by Fiona Adamczewski who has a great deal of experience in promoting the work of craftsmen. She consequently has a sympathetic understanding of their aims and ambitions, their ups and their downs, and was therefore the obvious person to write this book for the Embroiderers' Guild.

Elizabeth Benn
Chairman, The Embroiderers' Guild.

POLYANTHUS

ELIZABETH ASHURST

Elizabeth Ashurst has always enjoyed working on an architectural
scale, feeling that it enables her to express fully her feeling for
colour, surface texture and movement, within the framework of a
grid. She acknowledges stained glass, glass bottles, glass-houses,
some contemporary painters, Indian textiles and the forms and
colours of nature and architecture as her major influences and
chooses to work in materials such as dyed silk 'to create maximum
luminosity and to avoid the heaviness associated with tapestry'.

'Polyanthus' is an expression of the dynamic balance between
nature and technology. It is a synthesis of her studies based on
colour analyses, drawings and photographs, ranging from
flowers to stained glass, modern architecture, peasant
embroidery and tapestry weaving and was composed of strips of
her own dyed silk, hand-stitched onto canvas.

Elizabeth Ashurst completed a diploma in textile art at
Goldsmiths' College, London, in 1985. Prior to this she had gained
a City and Guilds Certificate, Part I, in embroidery at
Hammersmith College and Southampton College in 1969,
followed by Part II, taken part-time, at Goldsmiths' College and
Southampton College in 1971. In 1983 she became Chairman of
the East Surrey branch of the Embroiderers' Guild.

BURGH ISLAND

JAN BEANEY

Jan Beaney was trained initially as a painter and the effect of light in the landscape is a continuing preoccupation, showing itself in much of her textile work. Burgh Island, off the Plymouth coast, has often been a source of inspiration, as she and her family have spent many happy holidays there. She came away each time with drawings, photographs and notes to serve as reminders. The textures of the landscape are her main preoccupation: in order to express the contrast between lichen- and moss-covered rocks and the dense overhanging foliage of Burgh Island she has evolved a particular way of working.

Jan works on a base of spun algernate, a dissolvable fabric, onto which she bonds various fabrics using Bond-a-web. The individual shapes are linked with machine-stitching and the whole piece is then boiled to dissolve the algernate. This method affords her the possibility of producing stitch effects suggestive of the thread-like mosses, ferns and grasses and the delicate tracery of fine branches masking the more solid rock forms beneath. In some instances she works over the surface with machine- and hand-stitchery to further emphasise or blend the shapes and textures employed. An additional bonus is the possibility of having an uneven edge to the final piece.

Jan Beaney's face is familiar to thousands of people who watched her very successful appearance on television; in 1980 when she presented the BBC TV series *Embroidery*, ten programmes showing new aspects of design employing a number of embroidery techniques; and in 1985 when she presented a mini series on *Pebble Mill at One* on ideas for design in embroidery.

She has taught ever since 1959 and is currently teaching City and Guilds embroidery courses at Windsor and Maidenhead College of Further Education in conjunction with her friend and colleague, Jean Littlejohn.

Jan has been a member of the '62 Group since 1963 and has shown in all their exhibitions both in the UK and abroad. She is also the author of a number of books and has had articles published in numerous magazines in Britain and the United States.

Married, with two children, she lives in Maidenhead, successfully combining a hectic domestic life with a diverse career involving not only teaching, writing and television presentation, but the role of examiner for City and Guilds, executive committee membership of the Embroiderers' Guild and presidency of the Windsor and Maidenhead branch of the Embroiderers' Guild.

PLUMBAGO

RICHARD BOX

Flowers are a constantly recurring theme in Richard Box's work. The countryside of Sussex where he was born and grew up may have been the prime influence. He works directly from nature, drawing and painting in situ and taking numerous photographs to serve as an aide-memoire.

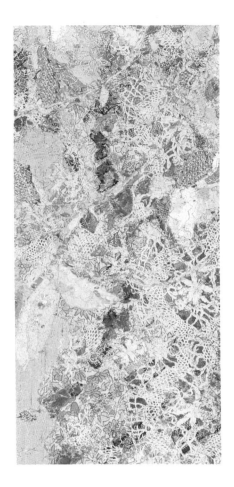

A number of watercolours and oil paintings of plumbago acted as a stimulus for the embroidery illustrated here. He made an enlarged drawing to ensure the balance of the design as a whole and to serve as a template and a stencil. He applied many small pieces of a variety of materials to a 'backing' fabric with glue and completed the process with hand- and machine-embroidery.

Richard Box trained as a painter, first at Hastings School of Art and later at Goldsmiths' College, London. He pursues his interest in painting concurrently with the development of his textile art and tends to include both types of work in his exhibitions.

After many years of teaching he has recently 'retired' in order to devote all his time to the development of his own work. He has always enjoyed teaching and plans to continue involvement with workshops and day-schools throughout the country.

His interest in textiles was encouraged by Constance Howard whom he met while doing a post-graduate course in art teaching at Goldsmiths' College. She urged him to experiment with stitching techniques using both hand-sewing and a machine.

Richard is a member of the '62 Group and has exhibited with them in the United Kingdom and abroad, his work being included in the 1984 British Textile Art exhibition in Japan. In 1981 he appeared in the BBC TV series *Embroidery* and he is one of the twelve artists included in *Twelve British Embroiderers*, a publication which was released in 1984 and followed by an exhibition of the same name in Japan in the autumn of 1985.

He lives in a flat in a fine Regency terrace house overlooking the common at Blackheath. His large, elegant drawing-room with its huge sash windows commanding a view of the garden, is crowded with examples of his own work, with old family portraits and with the work of other artists whom he admires.

Richard Box has recently completed work on a book – 'aimed at helping the "fearful" develop their own ideas for embroidery design' he says, pulling one of his familiar self-deprecatory faces. He has always been a popular, sympathetic lecturer and teacher and clearly his experience in this field has provided him with a rich source of material.

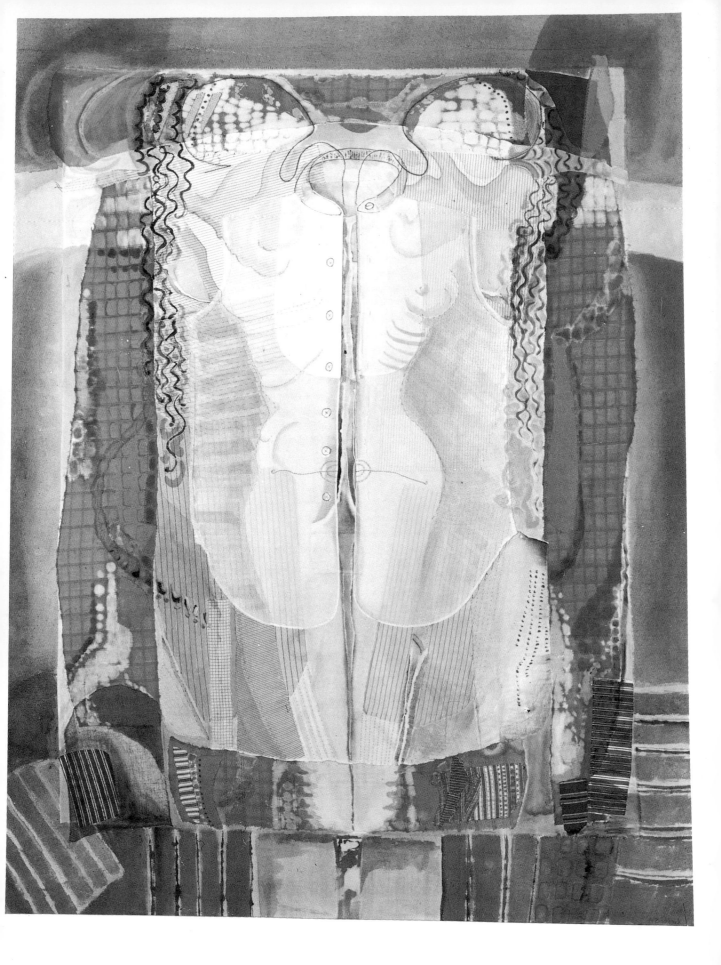

TIRESIAS

AUDREY BROCKBANK

Shirts appear frequently in Audrey Brockbank's work because she feels them to be a strong symbol of the person. Everything she does is a celebration of the man and the woman in each of us, implying conflict, duality and ambiguity. Her work is the result of her own personal experience and view of life. For her, shirts lend themselves so much to creativity as things can be packed into them, they can cloak things or reveal things, and this particular piece is a joyous evocation of these ideas.

As one would expect in someone with a background of painting, Audrey Brockbank works from drawings. She does many, but she likes to feel that in each work there comes a moment when the materials take over, when the work grows intuitively. Her way of working is very simple. Shapes are cut out and applied to a background, using straight stitching., She dyes her own materials using both chemical and natural dyes, and she says that her work always involves the use of a large quantity of paint.

Audrey Brockbank trained as a painter. It was not until 1977, when she completed a year's teaching at Whitelands College (now the Roehampton Institute) for a tutor who was on a sabbatical, that she became interested in textiles. Her period of teaching coincided with the change of Whitelands into the Roehampton Institute and she was encouraged to diversify. She took a four-day course in textiles at Winchester and since that time her interest in textiles has grown. From 1980 to 1982 she pursued a postgraduate diploma in art and design (textiles) at Goldsmiths' College, London, consolidating that interest. She still paints, however, as a visit to the bright, spacious studio apartment she shares with her husband proves. On a grey, wintry day, lunching there off bright yellow Italian ceramic plates, surrounded by looms, easels, paintings and textiles and the multitudinous gleanings of two visually obsessed people, it is easy to forget that what lies beyond the four walls is Chiswick and not the Chianti!

In 1983 Audrey secured a Crafts Council grant to aid her in the pursuit of a new preoccupation, ikat. She believes that it is a good thing for artists not to be confined to one discipline because they feed off each other.

A CAST OF THOUSANDS

MICHAEL BRENNAND–WOOD

It is tempting to speculate on the probability that Michael Brennand-Wood's childhood in the weaving town of Bury influenced his decision to opt for the medium of textiles. His grandmother taught him to knit and sew as a child, mainly to keep him busy on rainy days, but he doubts that these early family influences stood heavily on the scales when it came to his choice of medium. He explains that he completed two foundation years and as a result was able to combine various disciplines during the second of these years. By the time he came to choose his field of specialisation he had already identified the particular areas he wished to investigate and, on looking into the possibilities offered by the various departments at Manchester Polytechnic, he concluded that he would be best served by following a course in embroidery. Almost inevitably, he was the only male student on the course, but he did not find this a disadvantage. His tutors were encouraging and he was forceful enough to bend the system to accommodate his more outlandish experiments.

He began by investigating the physical structure of the stitch, using simple wooden frames or grids as a basis for the threads and moved on to incorporate mobile units. He became known rapidly for the eclectic and controversial nature of his productions, the range of which have included pieces small enough to qualify for inclusion in the series of international miniature textiles exhibitions and, at the other end of the scale, as large as 27 × 6ft (8 × 1.8m), employing materials such as acrylics, paper, threads, wood and fabric.

'Cast of Thousands' was completed in September/October 1986 and measures 6 × 6 × 1ft (1.8 × 1.8 × 0.3m). Technically, the work is essentially a painted relief into which fabric and thread have been incorporated. The materials employed are wood, acrylics, fabric, wire, threads and paper collage.

Over the last two years Michael has been interested in the relationship between a single object or a group of objects and the wall surface against which they are viewed. For this piece he decided to construct his own 'wall surface' and relate the fragmented circle accordingly. His intention was to make a work which was theatrical in content, physical in appearance and which explored the use of a three-dimensional line. Influences are notoriously difficult to identify, but he cites micro-imagery, musical notation, landscape and archaeology as major sources of inspiration.

Michael Brennand-Wood was born in Bury, Lancashire. He completed a BA (Hons) in textiles at Manchester Polytechnic in 1975 and an MA in textiles at Birmingham Polytechnic in 1976. He is currently lecturing at Goldsmiths' College, London, and lives in Wrestlingworth, Bedfordshire, where he maintains his studio.

He has exhibited widely in Britain, Germany, Holland, Belgium, Poland, Switzerland, Australia, New Zealand, the United States, Japan and Zimbabwe, and has work in public collections in London at the Victoria and Albert Museum, the Crafts Council Collection and the Contemporary Art Society Collection; in the Museum of Modern Art, Kyoto, Japan, and in many Australian collections.

In 1984 he spent six months' residency at the Western Australian Institute of Technology, Perth.

He has been the recipient of a number of grants and awards, including a Crafts Council grant in 1978.

FIRE OVER WOOD, DRESDEN

JULIA CAPRARA

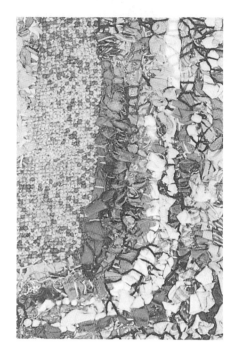

In 1976 the dress designer David Butler saw a hanging by Julia Caprara in an exhibition. This hanging was based on the textures of snow and frost in a winter garden and was heavily stitched, combining fabric strips and densely textured woollen areas. It prompted David Butler to commission Julia to use the technique to embroider a series of evening dresses and shawls. He showed these, with great success, in Paris and the USA and there followed a period when she became intensely and successfully involved in the world of fashion design, at first an exciting and stimulating experience, but ultimately one which she found to be totally exhausting. A new refinement in her technique was a direct result of this association, but she was finally driven to the realisation that the intense pressures involved in the fashion business were not something she could adapt to. She returned to making individual textile pieces and, during a severe, somewhat protracted illness, evolved a method of working intensively on small components which could be stitched together to form a whole.

In her current work she combines hand- and machine-embroidery with mixed media, applied paint and dye. She works at home, her small studio watched over by a slender, green, goggle-eyed chameleon who lives in a miniature tank-contained jungle.

Her most recent series, 'Colour Sounds', includes the piece 'Fire over Wood, Dresden'. This series was made in response to various violent incidents in recent world history, the bombing of Dresden being the source of inspiration for the piece illustrated here. In creating this work she referred to the I Ching and the hexagram that presented itself ran:

> Fire over wood
> The image of the caldron
> Thus the superior man consolidates his fate
> By making his position correct.

Julia Caprara attended Hornsey College of Art, completing a National Diploma in Design in stained glass and wood engraving in 1960. She followed this with an Art Teacher's Certificate in 1961. After leaving college she taught in various schools and from 1964 to 1968 was Head of the Art Department in the Henrietta Barnett School. From 1970 to the present day she has been a freelance teacher, tutoring short courses in a variety of situations, including a lecture tour of Japan.

Julia Caprara is a member of the '62 Group, acting as Publicity Secretary (1972–4), as Exhibitions Secretary (1977–8) and as Chairman (1980–5). In 1984 she accompanied the '62 Group exhibition to Japan. She has exhibited widely both at home and abroad and has work in public and private collections in the UK, the USA, Canada, Japan and Israel. In 1980 she participated in the BBC TV series *Embroidery*, presented by Jan Beaney.

SCAFFOLDING

JO BUDD

During her time at the University of Newcastle-upon-Tyne, Jo Budd specialised in painting and it was only when a love affair with American patchwork quilts familiarised her with a technique that seemed suited to the geometric forms of her choice, that she turned to the use of textiles in her work. Her main concerns have always been those of colour, light and form in the 'painterly' sense. Cloth allowed her to experiment with large areas of plain colour with more freedom than was possible using paint.

Her first figurative textile pieces were based largely on architectural subjects, the straight lines and geometric shapes lending themselves easily to the sewn technique. The limitations of the materials have, in some manner, dictated ways of approaching a subject and this, in turn, has prompted new techniques.

As her initial interest was with colour she evolved a way of stretching the material flat and sewing from the back in order to avoid the distraction of shadows which, she felt, would interfere with the colour values. Since those early attempts her interest in the textural qualities of the cloth itself has grown and she has moved on to dyeing her own fabrics.

She now works with cut, dyed 'scraps', pinning them directly to a backing, allowing the raw, frayed edges to show. The picture surface is frequently textured by loose ends hanging off it. In this she has been influenced by a growing preoccupation with the weathered and decaying surfaces of walls.

'Scaffolding' was one of a series of pieces Jo created, based on architectural subjects. The bulk of these works appeared in an exhibition entitled 'On the Wall' at the Ceolfrith Gallery in the Sunderland Arts Centre in July 1985.

The original starting point for this piece was a building Jo had seen 'wrapped' in safety nets and with scaffolding erected. Shafts of sunlight were falling across and through the nets, obscuring the building completely with only the geometry of the scaffolding to suggest the underlying structure. She did not work directly from a photograph, as she had done in the past, but merely used the colour range to start dyeing various scraps and larger chunks of material, using wax and paste resist techniques and sponging on 'proceon' dyes to get a suitable textured effect. Working in this way, she finds that when the fabric pieces are washed out, the selection procedure commences and she finally uses only about half of the material she has dyed in preparation.

She starts by pinning the pieces directly onto the 'backing' material, working on one area at a time and balancing colours and shapes as she goes along. As soon as there is something on the backing the next piece of material is made to 'work' with that. She only refers back to the original source if she is stuck and things are not going right or to refresh her memory.

In 'Scaffolding' Jo found herself exploring the counterpoint between the thin lines of the scaffolding structure and the less precise, but nonetheless geometric forms of the background where textures and tones produced a type of blurring or softening of the geometry. When a thin stripe of one colour passes over areas of colour lighter and darker than itself she observed that the optical effect was to make the stripe recede and then come forward again. She was interested in the suggestion of a drawn perspective in the thin lines of the scaffolding and the aerial perspective of the softer shapes of the background. Ultimately, the piece is about balance between colours, shapes, tonal areas and line as opposed to 'flat' areas. Her aim was to express the harmony she had seen in the subject.

Along the Same Lines III

BEVERLEY CLARK

During her second year at Goldsmiths' College, London, Beverley Clark completed a one-day course in smocking. 'From that day on I've done nothing but pleating,' she confesses. She was somewhat dissatisfied with textiles and had begun to consider moving to a fine arts course, but in considering the available alternatives found that nothing quite satisfied her. For a long time she had wanted to do something 'structured' but somehow the means eluded her. The smocking course provided the solution.

Her preference has always been for the monochrome. Colour exercises very little appeal and her three-dimensional totems in pleated calico and canvas have become the pale, dramatic presences by which she is best known. These have grown out of an abiding interest in cathedral architecture. Her work crosses the boundary between craft and fine art and belongs to no immediately recognisable tradition.

The two-dimensional piece 'Along the Same Lines' was a departure, to some extent, inspired by her first visit to Venice taken during the Easter vacation in 1985. The receding perspective and extraordinary geometry of the piece is indubitably urban in connotation, echoing images of Piero's ideal city.

Her method of working grew out of a desire to produce a quality in the material suggestive of age. Old fabrics have an appeal, she believes, just because they are worn, because time and the elements have transformed them, replacing their starchy freshness with a richer, more evocative quality to which we respond.

To produce the effects seen in her pieces she resorts to an extraordinary process. Working with calico or canvas she begins by applying a coat of diluted emulsion to the 'right' side of the material. With a preconceived design plan in mind she then proceeds to machine-sew pleats into the material and finally applies wood-stain to the reverse side of the piece. When this action is completed she unpicks the stitching and repeats the entire process as many times as possible until the resistance in the fabric begins to break down. By this method she arrives at that elusive quality in the fabric which we perceive in antique cloth.

Recently she has begun to work in ceramics and it is interesting to speculate on the possible direction her work might take, combining the different materials perhaps to produce yet another form.

TIGER PROTECTOR

SUE BULL

Sue Bull has chosen to work in the textile idiom as she feels that textile art is the most accessible form of art, the easiest for people to relate to, particularly if it is functional. 'Tiger Protector' was intended as a bedspread, 'throw' or wall-hanging.

Everyone has contact with textiles. Perhaps it is easier for people to imagine having them around all the time, rather than 'fine art' which seems to scare a lot of people! I have this theory that most couples, when they lie in bed, lie in the same way – the woman on the right, the man on the left. So the vicious-looking black tiger was the female, the playful one on his back, the male. I suppose it was how I felt at the time. The sun and the moon hanging from the bottom are symbolic, too. The female symbol is the moon. The nervous little eye looking in horror at the scene is a self-portrait. It's me hiding behind the patchwork in the top left-hand corner. The quilt was originally for me, or another woman, as a protector and a reminder.

Sue Bull has no particular method of working and enjoys attempting everything. In this particular piece the work is bleached, dyed, painted and embroidered. The animals are appliquéd onto a velvet background and she has used both hand- and machine-stitching. All her work is based on her dreams and fantasies. Tigers appear frequently in Sue's work because she discovered that both she and her mother were born in the Chinese year of the tiger.

Sue Bull completed a BA(Hons) in textiles at Goldsmiths' College, London, in 1985 and since 1986 has been on a government enterprise scheme.

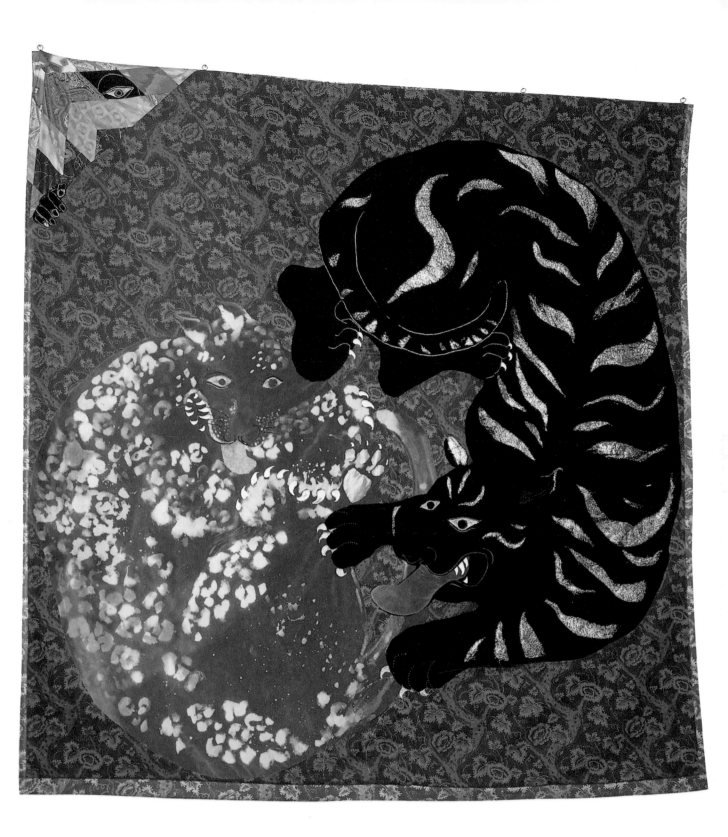

POWER

BERYL DEAN, MBE

The secular panel 'Power' was inspired by the National Westminster Bank's building in the City of London which Beryl Dean feels symbolises the wealth of the City. She wanted to contrast this power of wealth with the strength of industry which she symbolised by iron and steel smelting, atomic, electrical and water power.

The panel was made from scraps of silk ties and was carried out in blind appliqué with a certain amount of hand-stitching. There are areas of patchwork where each facet reflects the light differently. This was partly determined of necessity as some of the scraps were awkward shapes. Small units such as windows were made from various woven patterns in silks. Certain details were made from shapes cut in card, wrapped with 'filo floss' silk and applied. The panel was designed to hang on the walls of a boardroom or head office and took almost seven months to complete.

Beryl Dean received her training at the Bromley School of Art and the Royal School of Needlework, London. Over the years she has taught at a number of schools of art and adult education institutes and has lectured throughout Britain and in the USA.

In 1956, having come to the conclusion that ecclesiastical embroidery was not keeping pace with the developments being manifested in secular embroidery, she resolved to concentrate all her energies on an attempt to infuse new concepts and disciplines into this particular branch of the craft. Her training at the Royal School of Needlework had provided her with a thorough schooling in the techniques of traditional embroidery and her constant involvement with art schools had kept her exposed to developments in the field of design. She felt, therefore, that she was uniquely equipped to effect the desired change.

Her first step was to organise an exhibition of ecclesiastical embroidery at the Royal College of Art, London, and this event coincided with the launching of her first book, followed by five further books on different aspects of the subject.

The first courses in church embroidery were initiated at Hammersmith College of Art, members of the classes producing work for their own churches and taking part in projects under Beryl Dean's direction. Examples of this were the 'Hammersmith Copes', the 'Jubilee Cope' for St Paul's Cathedral, London, and the huge hanging for Chelmsford Cathedral. Interest in the subject grew and led to lecture tours and exhibitions both in London and abroad.

Beryl Dean's life-long mission to improve the standards of ecclesiastical embroidery earned her an MBE (Member of British Empire). She was also awarded an ARCA (Associate Royal College of Art) and is a Fellow of the Society of Designer Craftsmen.

CAVE PAINTING

SARAH BUNGEY

Sarah Bungey has never visited the cave paintings of Lascaux or the bushmen paintings of southern Africa but, inevitably, her work calls them to mind. 'Cave Painting' is executed on a Vilene base in free machine-stitching, stencils, spray-painting and sealing wax. She has always enjoyed taking advantage of the many different materials and techniques available to anyone working in the textile medium and uses whatever is necessary to create the effect she requires.

Sarah Bungey was born in Essex and trained at Winchester School of Art, graduating with First Class Honours in printed textiles in 1976. She went on to the Royal College of Art, London, to complete a degree by project between 1976 and 1978. From 1978 to 1981 she worked at the Royal College as a part-time research fellow, carrying out research into decorative treatments of wool. From 1979 to 1980 she worked as a part-time fabric consultant to a company of interior designers in Pimlico, London.

She has been the recipient of a number of awards, including a Sanderson's travel scholarship enabling her to spend ten weeks visiting art schools and textile firms in the United States of America, a Crafts Council equipment grant and an Eastern Arts maintenance grant.

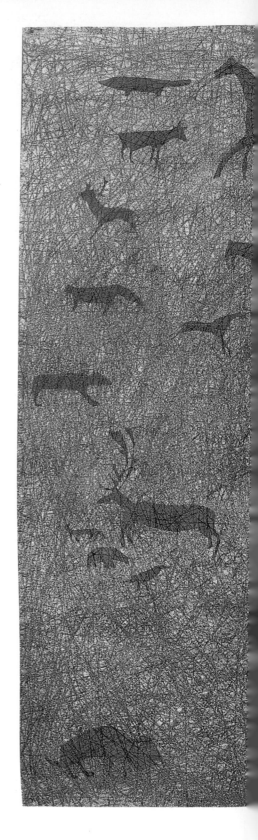

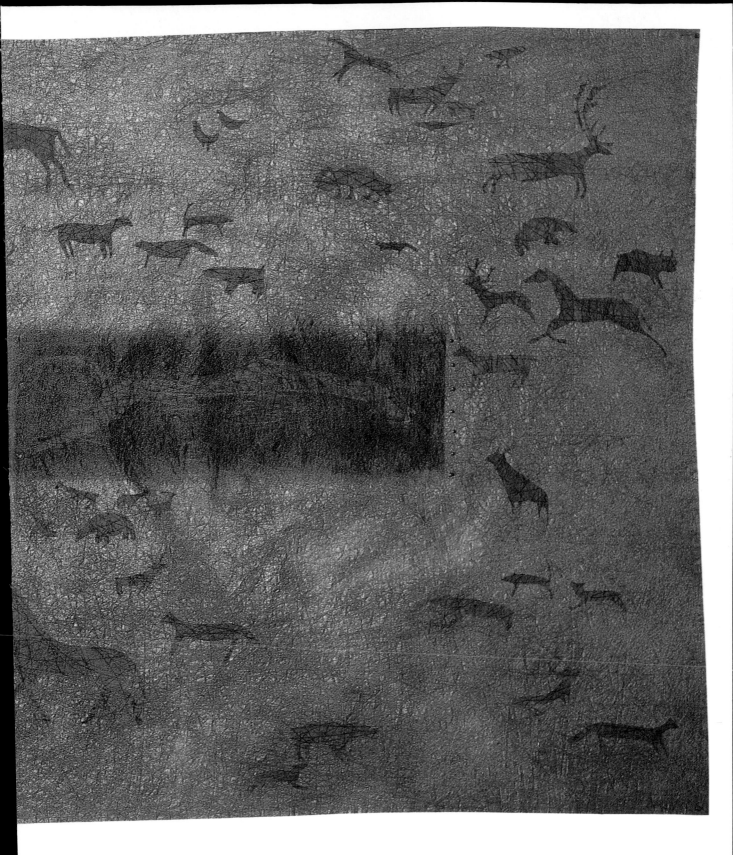

THE RED CENTRE OF AUSTRALIA

MARY FOGG

The piece entitled 'The Red Centre of Australia' was inspired by the ten days that Mary Fogg spent in a campervan near Alice Springs in the middle of Australia. She had already flown over this vast desert several times with her eyes glued to the window and the colour, the vastness and the untamed quality of the desert were overwhelming to one whose life has been based on the cared-for fertility of England.

She set out to express something of her impressions in pieced textile form. She started, as she always does, with a small-scale fabric collage and then set about experiments in technique and materials. She rejected her usual method of quilted strips with edges hidden because she wanted something rougher and more untidy, but within her personal definition of a quilt which must be able to withstand handling without damage.

This work has raw-edged overlapping strips of mixed cottons and silks applied to a soft woollen interlining and cotton backing with frequent lines of fairly irregular machining.

Mary Fogg was trained at the Malvern School of Art and at the Slade School, London.

AUTUMN IN ARDBRECKNISH

ROSEMARY CAMPBELL

Much of the inspiration for Rosemary Campbell's work is derived from the landscape. 'Autumn in Ardbrecknish' is named after the remote and secluded spot on the shores of Loch Awer, in the west of Scotland, where the countryside is lush and rich in colour, particularly in autumn. Most of her drawings and photographic references are collected during her holidays and developed in the subsequent months.

The use of multiple surfaces and transparent fabrics to create depth and distance has fascinated her for some time, in addition to combining modern and traditional techniques. 'Autumn in Ardbrecknish' is comprised of these elements.

The upper layer combines silk with painted organdie. The leafy background is created by applying crushed and machine-embroidered magazines on which leaves, created by machining using natesh and metallic threads and dissolvable fabric, are superimposed. The branches are covered cane which intertwines and pierces the surface of the painted organdie to reappear in a different area. The pool of water is stitched in shadow work and holes are burned in the organdie to reveal the surface below.

Rosemary Campbell attended the Duncan of Jordanstone College of Art in Dundee, obtaining a diploma in painted textiles and embroidery in 1967. Since 1980 she has been a lecturer in embroidery at Telford College of Further Education in Edinburgh. Her work is represented in the collection of the Royal Museum of Scotland.

SILKEN STRIPES

HANNAH FREW PATERSON

From a very early age Hannah Frew Paterson was interested in embroidery and knitting which she learnt from her mother. At art school she experimented with methods of producing raised, layered and structured forms and this interest remained with her. In some instances it becomes a form of textile engineering, building one embroidered surface on another. She devised systems whereby fabrics could be used to create shapes and forms, involving the effect of light on their surfaces.

Because of her teaching commitments she has always had only a limited amount of time to devote to her personal textile work. Much of her time has been taken up in executing various commissions for churches. This type of work, however, has acted as a discipline and provided her with the opportunity to experiment with various materials and methods.

She does a great deal of drawing, but feels that this, too, is an indirect rather than a direct source of stimulation.

Hannah's chief area of interest within embroidery has always been related in some way to the three-dimensional qualities of fabrics and thread. Recently she has investigated the possibilities of designing with large-scale stitchery, using her own hand-spun silk threads which range from a regular or normally large thread to one which measures approximately 1in (25mm) in diameter, resulting in stitches almost 4in (100mm) in size. 'Silken Stripes' developed from this original idea, but also involved another aspect of textiles which intrigues her, namely the integration of hand-weaving, spinning and embroidery.

The inspiration for the embroidery came from studies of an old semi-submerged boat on the shore. The ribs of the boat on the inside stood out sharply against the mixture of stones, sand and seaweed which was caught in the bottom of the boat, creating a textural pattern. From this idea the design developed into a weave structure incorporating a strip of double cloth weaving which was eventually stiffened by inserting a length of perspex down the stripe to form a 'rib'. Large-scale hand-spun silk threads were partly woven into the structure and then left free until the woven area was completed. When the weaving, which had a dyed warp grading from natural white to a dark neutral, was removed from the loom, each panel was stretched on a frame to enable the hand-stitching to be carried out, creating the desired textural pattern between the ribs. Each panel was stiffened at the top and bottom to make it hang in an angled shape so that when tensioned into the frame they took up a zig-zag formation, to heighten the effect of light on the stitched surface.

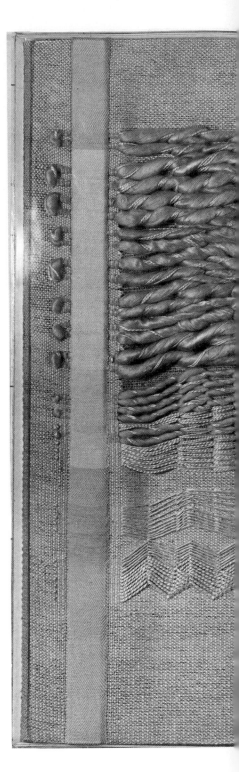

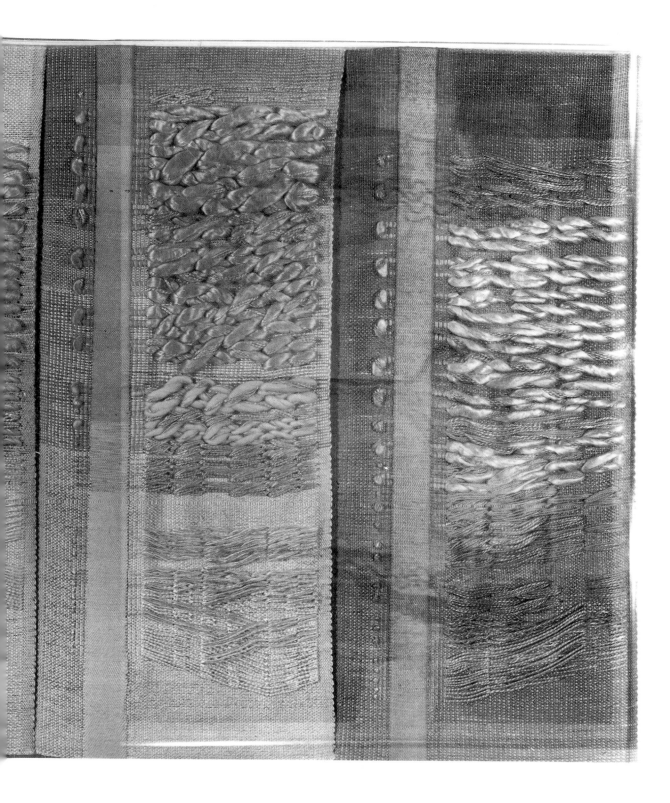

SELF-PORTRAIT

MARY COZENS-WALKER

Visitors to the 1986 Embroiderers' Guild exhibition were startled by a life-like, but larger-than-life face staring out at them from the inside of a 'cupboard'. The face was that of Mary Cozens-Walker who was frequently present 'in the flesh' as if to endorse the accuracy of her textile self-portrait. Tall and vividly good-looking, Mary has made a reputation as the producer of quirky three-dimensional textile pieces. Her self-portrait was instantly purchased by the Arts Council.

According to Mary's husband, the painter Antony Green, the piece was arresting because 'Mary jolly well knows how to draw!' She was trained as a painter and it was not until 1981 that she began a postgraduate diploma in embroidery and textiles.

Mary is often quoted as saying that everything she makes is a celebration of the places and people she loves. She and her husband met at art school and married as soon as they left. Their marriage has been celebrated in paint again and again by Antony Green and Mary's evocation of the places and atmospheres of their happy life together, executed in her case in stitch, seems part of a delicately balanced double-act. When in London they live in a crowded flat in an old building off the Highgate Road where Antony Green has lived most of his life, but whenever possible they visit their cottage in Cambridgeshire.

Their cottage has been immortalised in stitch by Mary, every tiny detail meticulously executed and the family's life laid bare on one side of the building where the rooms are opened up to reveal their two daughters crouching before a fire and the pair of them lying in bed in the morning sunlight. No family life has ever been more thoroughly documented; they have recorded every event and every protagonist, and their unashamed delight in each other, in their daughters and even in their dotty, pigeon-toed fox-terrier, Rosie, is both enviable and infectious. Mary has found a medium to suit her through which she can communicate her joie de vivre and is delighted to have done so.

When it came to creating a piece for the Embroiderers' Guild exhibition, she was presented with a challenge. Customarily she works in the round, but the requirement was for a wall-hung piece. Accordingly, she hit upon the device of making a three-dimensional face in a cupboard, to be hung on the wall. The face was painted with acrylics onto calico and embroidered with straight stitches in stranded cottons. It was then cut out and mounted on a second sheet of calico which was stuffed from the back by slashing the backing cloth and packing it with polyester wadding. Definition was created by quilting from the front. The hair was embroidered with longer stitches in stranded cottons, but to achieve greater texture she laid strands of weaving wool on top of this. The background was painted with acrylics and the whole image was then laced to a piece of hardboard and screwed into position from the back of the cupboard.

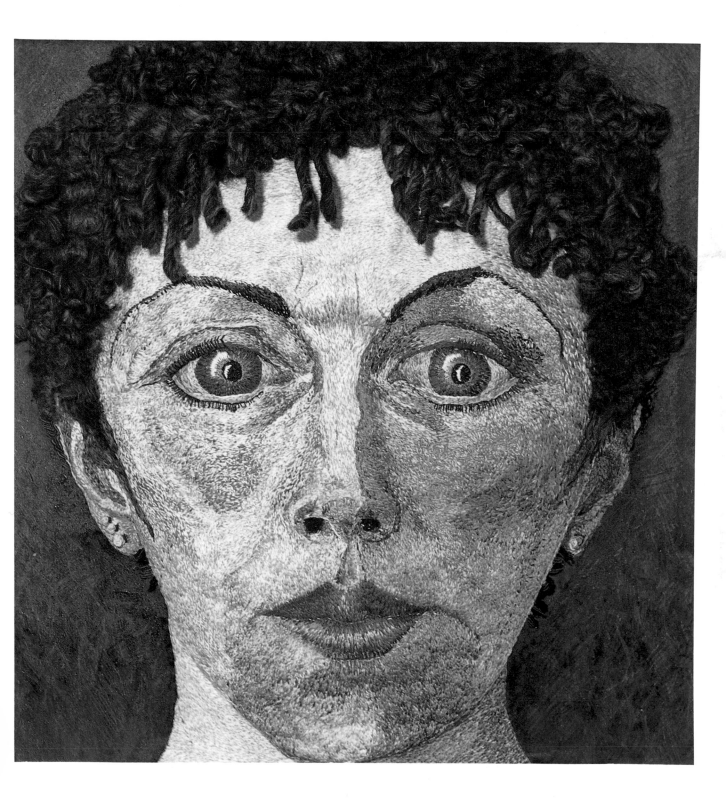

Untitled

GAVIN FRY

Gavin Fry sits in his small box-like studio high up in a vast council block in South London and suffers the onslaught of his large black and white cat Rosie. Small, mercurial and puckish, he is a perfect match for his feline antagonist. His bright eyes, circled by large round spectacles, sparkle and blink while he talks animatedly about his work. Beyond the window the vast sprawl of London disciplines itself into an infinite pattern of lights in the gathering darkness of the winter evening. Rosie, whose name belies his sex, explores the surface of a large textile lying on the floor and finally settles on the face of its subject.

It is probably the last piece that Gavin will do in that particular genre. He created it as an exercise in drawing because he felt that his drawing had become too tight. The background is 100 per cent rayon which he chose in order to present a very sad, stark subject set against a rich background. The figure was composed from numerous photographs so the result is more of a collage than a portrait of an individual. The outline is stitched very simply using a series of stitches – running stitch, chain stitch and a type of satin stitch – which he makes up as he goes along. He made a flour and water paste to use as dye resist and sometimes bleach is incorporated into the mixture.

All around the cerulean-coloured walls Gavin has tacked up a series of miniature portraits on which he has begun to work. Some are completed, others are mere sketches and there are little preparatory drawings. This is the direction his work is taking, although it is a return to something he began to explore when he was a student at Goldsmiths' College, London. He is working here on a very small scale and the pieces are densely stitched in contrast to previous work. 'It's really stump-work, I suppose,' he says with a shrug that is almost dismissive, but the vivid little presences stare out with all the assertiveness of large portraits in a gallery – each one surrounded by symbols and personal paraphernalia. There is an incomplete self-portrait surrounded by small silver skulls and a finished self-portrait where the jaunty, bespectacled face emerges from a dense conglomeration of 'printed' surfaces – every minute word legible. What is to come, one feels, promises to be even more interesting, more his own thing, than what has already been seen.

Map Form I

JEAN DAVEY-WINTER

Jean Davey-Winter works mainly with recycled computer paper. She dyes the paper at the first stage and subsequently adds fragments of yarns, fabrics and other types of paper. These processes are followed by printing onto the paper, using etching techniques and the print marks are finally reinforced with stitches, echoing their forms. Paint and crayon are frequently employed to enrich the surface still further.

Most of her work is a response to travel experience, to impressions of particular environments. Like the maps they resemble, Jean Davey-Winter's pieces usually fold up and are easily transportable. 'Map Form I' is such a piece where a rich iconography carries with it powerful and mysterious associations.

Jean Davey-Winter completed a National Diploma in Design in printed textiles at Birmingham College of Art and Design in 1963. She was awarded Royal Society of Arts bursaries in printed furnishing textiles and laminated plastics in the same year and travelled extensively in Scandinavia. Part of her time there was spent working in a weaving studio in Fredrikstad, Norway.

For the next ten years, she worked as a freelance textile designer and part-time lecturer and from 1974 to 1979 as a full-time lecturer in foundation studies at Solihull College of Technology. In 1979 she moved to Oxford and began to work in mixed media. From 1982 to the present time she has been a part-time lecturer in foundation studies and printmaking at Buckinghamshire College, High Wycombe, and she is also a visiting lecturer at Ruskin School of Drawing and Fine Art, Oxford.

Jean Davey-Winter is a member of the '62 Group and has been its vice-chairman since 1985. Apart from exhibiting regularly with the '62 Group she exhibits on a regular basis with Fibre Art and with the Oxford Printmakers Co-operative.

Her work has been the subject of one-person exhibitions at the Peter Dingley Gallery in Stratford-upon-Avon in 1973, 1979 and 1983 and she has also had solo exhibitions at the Ingrid Presser Gallery in Wiesbaden, West Germany, and the Anderson o'Day Gallery in London and had work included in group exhibitions in the UK, the USA, West Germany and Japan.

Examples of her work have been purchased by the Museum of Modern Art, Kyoto, Japan, by the Contemporary Arts Society and are included in many private collections.

In 1985 she was commissioned to execute ten paper pieces for the new London offices of Electronic Data Systems of Dallas, Texas, USA, a commission negotiated by Anderson o'Day.

ELY WEST WALL

WEST WALL AT ELY

ESTHER GRAINGER

Esther Grainger trained as a painter, graduating from Cardiff School of Art in 1934. Fairly late in life she discovered the medium of embroidery. For this reason she thinks in terms of organic colour and line rather than exploiting the beautiful decorative possibilities of varied stitches, and keeps instead to the simplest and most flexible ones such as stem, back or running stitch. These make a line and texture element used freely across colour areas as a form of drawing.

Esther always works by hand and although this method of working is time-consuming she prefers it. She likes the slow rhythm because for her it is an essential part of what is to be produced. She prefers to suggest rather than to present richness of surface. For this reason she does not use metallic threads or materials, but prefers the matt surfaces of woollen, cotton and heavy silk fabrics which allow the colour to suggest gold or jewelled effects.

All her life she has loved Romanesque architecture and artefacts and most of the large hangings she has made in recent years are based on architectural themes. 'West Wall at Ely', although exemplifying this development in her work, is more representational in form and more mosaic-like in technique than her other work. For many years she has made drawings of Ely Cathedral. She points out that in this piece there is very little distortion in the drawing. 'The treatment aims at expressing the intensity and richness of the subject, partly by means of constant subtle colour changes across the surface. The design of most other pieces is freer, bringing together characteristic elements in a less representational way.'

INDIAN SQUARES

JEAN DRAPER

Until recently, land, sea and sky in areas she knows well have been the starting points for Jean Draper's work, but a growing interest in pattern was fuelled by a textile tour in India two years ago. This has resulted in the use of a new range of colours and in experimentation with metallic effects, including gold leaf, combined with stitchery.

'Indian Squares' was executed on a background of magenta Indian silk. The central area is a grid composed of twenty-eight multi-layered squares. These are made of hand-made paper with drawing and hand-stitchery, machine-embroidery on dissolvable fabric and a central raised square of gold leaf on heavily textured hand-made paper. There is a subtle variation in the colouring of the squares to give greater richness to the centre of the panel. The deep surrounding border is built up from scraps of silks, chiffons and organdie which have been over-stitched with layers of fine hand-stitching in reds, pinks and oranges. Small squares of decorated hand-made paper and gold-leaf covered silk are incorporated in the edge along with many fine loops of thread and suspended fragments of transparent fabrics. This and other pieces are an on-going exploration of themes and ideas which have developed from Jean's Indian experience.

The process of embroidery is as important to Jean as the finished result. She finds it satisfying and exciting to stitch into a fabric in a rhythmic manner, making textured marks. The stitches are simple, mostly straight, knots and loops, and depend upon variety of thread, colour and change of direction for interest. She aims to do more than decorate the background fabric, thinking in terms of making a complete fabric surface of intricacy and refinement, by criss-crossing layer upon layer of stitches in fine threads. She would like to think that the image obtained is pleasing at a distance and the dense fabric surface is interesting on close inspection. Additional depth, both physical and illusional, is given with fine loops and fragments of silks and chiffons suspended above the flatter stitchery.

Jean Draper completed a National Diploma in Design at Stratford College of Art in 1959 and an Art Teacher's Certificate at London University Institute of Education in 1960. From 1960 she taught in a number of schools and colleges of art and in 1968 she became Lecturer and later Senior Lecturer in Textiles at West Midland College of Higher Education. She joined the '62 Group in 1979, participating in all their exhibitions in Britain and Japan. She continues to teach in a freelance capacity nationwide and frequently runs courses at the Embroiderers' Guild, Hampton Court.

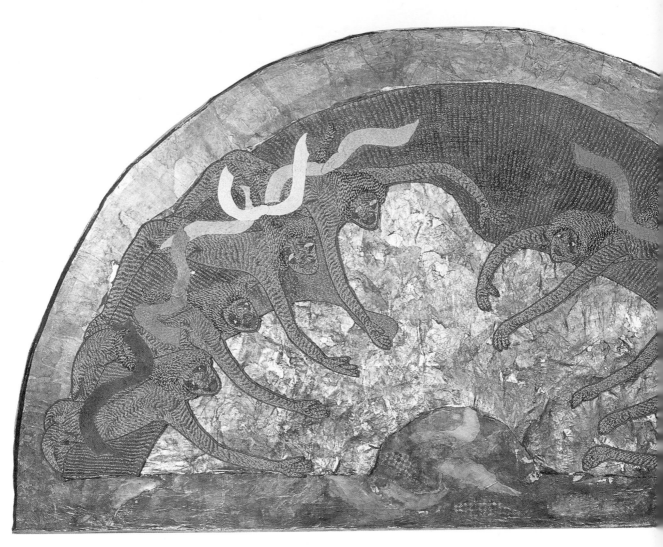

THE GOLD FISHERS

MARGARET HALL

Margaret Hall gew up on a farm in Hertfordshire. Her mother and grandmother both enjoyed knitting and her great-grandmother was a Hertfordshire lace-maker. These early family influences, coupled with meticulous training in formal embroidery techniques under a variety of tutors, including Constance Howard, Barbara Dawson and Christine Risley, have led to a disciplined attitude to hand-embroidery demonstrated most dramatically in the technical excellence of 'The Gold Fishers'.

This piece, the first stitched work Margaret Hall has produced for three years, is undoubtedly the finest example to date of a particular technique she has been evolving over the past few years. Padded shapes are couched over with gold thread to emphasise the figures. The use of minimal colour is deliberate.

Margaret confesses to a distinct dislike for the tradition of framing embroidery in imitation of painting. She has worked for some time on the conjunction of papier maché frames and embroidery and the result in the case of 'The Gold Fishers' is particularly effective. The labour-intensity of such work raises a definite problem when the matter of pricing the piece arises. Margaret worked so many man-hours on 'The Gold Fishers' that pricing her labour at the modest sum of £7 (approx $10) per hour resulted in a final asking price of £2,895 (approx $4,500).

Margaret Hall studied embroidery at Goldsmiths' College, London, obtaining a diploma in art and design in 1970. Since 1974 she has been a part-time teacher of embroidery at Goldsmiths' College and in 1979 she became a part-time teacher in the Textile Department of Bristol Polytechnic. These activities are augmented by involvement in numerous summer schools and short courses for local authorities, guilds and private groups throughout the country and in Canada and the USA.

RED-YELLOW-BLUE-RAZZLE-DAZZLE

ROSALIND FLOYD

Rosalind Floyd acknowledges that her work went through a crisis a few years ago when she felt that her inspiration had dried up and that somehow everything she did was becoming trivialised. She therefore resolved to explore new ways of working and began to make small things, rather like samples, concentrating on stitch and colour. She wanted to reduce everything to stitch and colour so that the subject of the piece became simplified to just that.

Out of this experimentation a new way of working evolved which is extremely painstaking and therefore time-consuming. 'Red-Yellow-Blue-Razzle-Dazzle' is the largest example of this method to date, each square in the piece taking her one hour to complete.

Her method of working is very slow. She prints a basic grid in black on white cloth and then, using three colours of thread, she covers the entire surface of the cloth with laid and couched work. In this piece, for example, using red, yellow and blue, she has produced a range of colours through the varying combinations of threads. Until 1980 all her work was 'framed', but now she is more interested in making embroideries which exploit the flexible qualities of the material. She aims at creating an image through 'stitchery' which could not be produced by any other method.

Rosalind Floyd completed a National Diploma in Design in textiles and embroidery at Leicester College of Art in 1958 and an advanced diploma in textiles at Goldsmiths' College, London, in 1975. She has taught continuously in one situation or another since 1958, taking a break only recently to concentrate on the completion of her submission to the 1986 Embroiderers' Guild exhibition. Currently she teaches three days a week at Goldsmiths' College. She has work in the Victoria and Albert Museum, London.

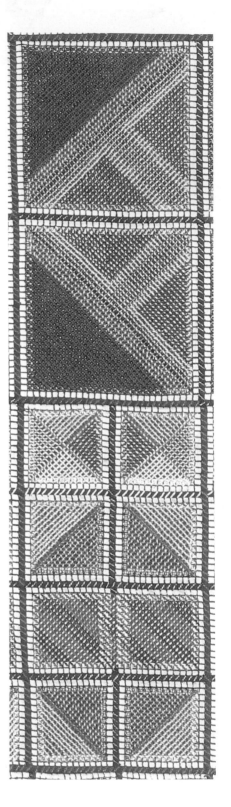

2500 SQUARES

ELIZABETH JANE HAPPS

The piece entitled '2500 Squares' is a development of Elizabeth Jane Happs' work in an area that she has been interested in for many years. She has always been fascinated by fabrics – by the way a cloth or hanging can be pieced and constructed together using decorative embroidery, printed, woven, quilted and applied fabrics, combined with constructed embroidery techniques. She has produced such fabrics in order to form garments, quilts and hangings.

Her designs evolve from ideas that come to her while she is drawing or painting landscapes – hence the watercolour 'painterly' quality reflected in the stitchery. It has never been her aim, however, to reflect landscape directly pictorially in embroidery. She has always looked for the form and strength in a landscape and these forms, shapes and strengths are what she interprets in a fabric piece, adding details in decorative embroidered areas.

She uses both the Bernina and the Cornely machines to construct her hangings and garments and occasionally employs vanishing muslin. Areas of quilting are an inherent part of all her fabric constructions. She feels that such areas add weight and strength to the pieces.

She is particularly concerned with the 'feel for cloth' of a fabric hanging because it has to work as a piece of fabric as well as a piece of textile and she believes that both are totally linked.

Elizabeth Jane Happs was trained at St Alban's School of Art and obtained a BA at Goldsmiths' College, London, in 1977, following this with an MA in textiles and fashion at Manchester Polytechnic in 1979. Since leaving college she has taught in a variety of secondary schools and served as an embroidery examiner for the GCE AEB Board. Her work has been included in exhibitions in the United Kingdom and the USA.

HIGH RISE

PATRICIA FOULDS

For many years Patricia Foulds' work has been concerned with the exploration of mathematical solutions in design and this has led, inevitably, to an interest in modern architecture.

'High Rise' was produced as part of a systematic investigation into design using a mathematical approach. It is not purely abstract, however, but based on forms visible in the modernist movement in architecture, derived from personal observations and photographs which she has taken in various parts of the world, with an emphasis on the Mediterranean area.

Far from being the depressing structures many people believe them to be, to Patricia they are things of beauty, often with a surrealist quality – elegant, giant monuments soaring into the sky. For her, they have a strange personal fascination and, particularly in a warm climate, a strong pattern element, changing from each viewpoint, which is emphasised by the clarity of light. Many are decorated with expensive materials both internally and externally and the colours, together with the silk fabrics used in the piece, were selected to reflect that mood. The design is not a copy of a building, but was evolved by taking a widely used basic pattern structure and carefully manipulating proportions and colour within in order to produce a cohesive whole, resulting in an image rather than a pattern which is suggestive of the structure of a high-rise building.

The work was designed to be used either as a decorative hanging or a quilt in a domestic scale interior or small office suite.

Patricia Foulds was trained at the West of England College of Art (1954–8) and at London University Institute of Education (1958–9). She has been senior tutor in charge of embroidery at Loughborough College of Art and Design since 1968.

THREE CROSSES

DIANA HARRISON

'Three Crosses' was one of a series of pieces that was born out of a
preoccupation with old buildings and the textures of crumbling
plaster, faded and cracked paintwork and weathered wood.
Diana Harrison has always drawn inspiration from architectural
sources. For a long time New York and its extraordinary buildings
were her chief preoccupation and much of her work was a
response to the interplay of architectural shapes and textures
encountered there, but lately she has become more interested in
older buildings and on a recent visit to Portugal she took
numerous photographs of doors, windows and walls in which her
interest in vivid juxtapositions of colour – blue, turquoise, red – is
revealed.

Now that she is once again buggy-walking a small baby, she has
discovered a whole host of new forms and textures to preoccupy
her in the crushed detritus of roads and gutters, the imprints of
litter that has been run over on road surfaces – cigarette packets,
book-matches, tin cans, and so on. She often visits a particular
beach in Kent where she collects litter thrown back by the sea and
this is now piling up in her studio – faded and disintegrating
wrappings and packages that 'have suffered a sea-change into
something rich and strange'. She thinks now of working with
paper and felting these objects into it.

She plans her work very deliberately, working on graph paper,
plotting the geometry of each piece. Nothing is random and she
does not work at all intuitively. There is always a preconceived
design idea which she aims for but, inevitably, during the process,
this alters.

Her first step, usually, is to spatter the surface of her fabric with
dye. This is followed by a steaming process and then parts of the
design are eaten away with discharge bleach. Then comes the
machine-stitching. The ends of the threads are dragged out and
tied and in some cases a further bleaching process may follow to
emphasise geometric shapes. It is quite deliberate and
meticulous.

The planning chest in her studio is full of drawings and sketch
books which reveal the thinking behind her work – precise,
delicate drawings of permutations of ideas, experiments with
other disciplines, even life drawings. There are the miniature
textiles which look back to a time when she worked on a smaller
scale and there are plans for larger pieces to come.

Diana Harrison completed a diploma in art and design at
Goldsmiths' College, London, in 1971 and went on to the Royal
College to follow an MA course in printed textiles from 1971 to
1973. At present she is a lecturer at West Surrey College of Art
and Design, Farnham, and, despite the pressures of combining
the roles of mother, wife and teacher, she declares that she is
determined to continue teaching. This is partly because she

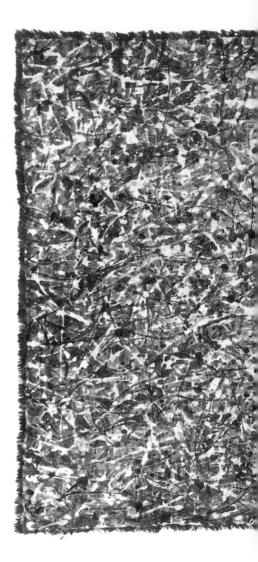

confesses to a real love of teaching but also because of the stimulation she derives from constant contact with other textile people and the catalytic atmosphere of a lively department. Her work has been bought by the Crafts Council, the Victoria and Albert Museum, London, and the Museum of Modern Art in Kyoto, Japan.

Split Circle Materials

SALLY FRESHWATER

Sally Freshwater completed a BA(Hons) in textiles at Goldsmiths' College, London, in 1980 and went on to do an MA at the Royal College of Art. She did not study embroidery at Goldsmiths' but found, in the freedom the course offered, an opportunity to develop her own interest in kites and Japanese paper constructions.

While at the Royal College of Art she discovered the work of Frei Otto. His cable-suspended tent constructions, seen to great advantage in the 1963 horticultural exhibition in Hamburg, at the German pavilion in the Montreal World Exhibition in 1967 and at the Olympics in Munich in 1972, fired her imagination. She began to work within similar disciplines, exploiting the use of repeated units, employing materials such as Vilene, silk, paper, cord and wire and investigating the potential of folded and collapsible constructions.

Her work involves precise arithmetical calculations and is painstakingly prepared on graph paper. Her formal mathematical studies ended with 'O' levels, but she has always had a natural aptitude for the subject and this is now coupled with a growing interest in the potential of computer-dictated design. While at the Royal College of Art she worked on a computer-designed project, but the facilities to effect its final implementation were not available at the college during her time.

Her father has always been a model-maker and although she doubts if this was a direct influence on the direction her work has taken, she is prepared to acknowledge that something may have rubbed off on her.

'Split Circle Materials' grew out of a series of drawn ideas which she had not been able to execute. It is again an exploration of geometrical relationships using Vilene, wood, thread and wire.

In recent years Sally has completed several interesting commissions, including a large-scale mobile for W. H. Smith's new branch at Swindon. This came about as a result of drawings she had included in a Hayward Gallery, London, annual British drawing exhibition in 1982. Smith's chose her work from a slide index of drawings maintained by the Arts Council which she finds gratifying as this indicates that her work would have been chosen in preference to that of professional sculptors.

Sally Freshwater's work was included in the 1982 fourth international exhibition of miniature textiles and in the international tapestry triennial in Lodz, Poland, in 1985–6 and has recently been included in a collection of work shown in Japan under the auspices of the Crafts Council. She has also exhibited in the Stor Gallery in Amsterdam.

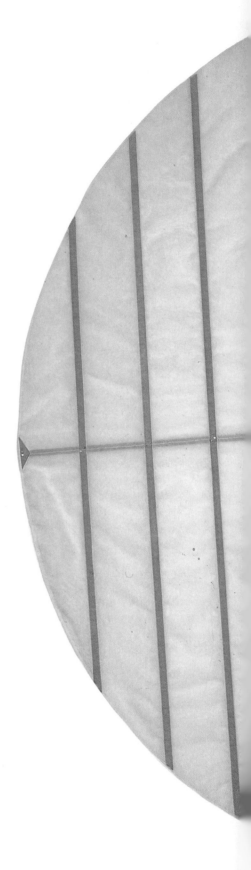

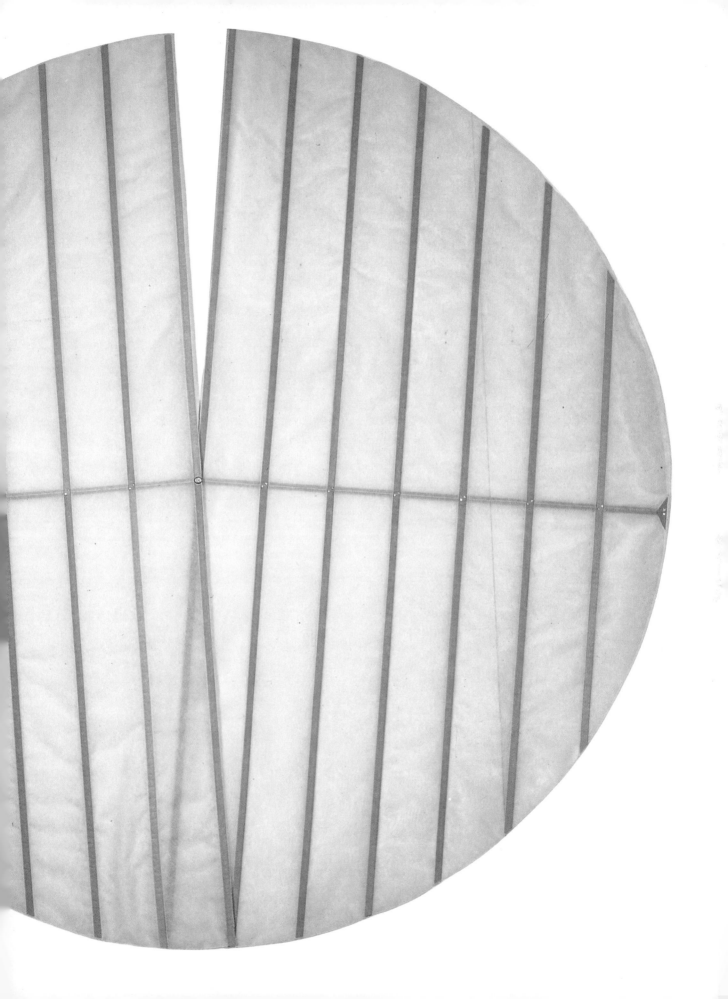

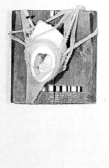

DECORATIONS

ROZANNE HAWKSLEY

Rozanne Hawksley was born in Portsmouth and remembers her grandmother, who lived near the entrance to the docks, stitching braid on sailors' shirts for a living. Her mother, too, was a needlewoman and very early in life she was initiated into the skills of stitchery.

Looking at the work she has produced across a lifetime, one is assailed by the dark vision underlying everything that Rozanne Hawksley does. It seems obvious that at one time or another she has had a love-hate relationship with Catholicism and equally obvious that she is wholly preoccupied with death and violence. The serious statements she chooses to make seem to stretch the medium in which she has chosen to make them almost to breaking point. Over the years she has continued to pursue the discipline of drawing and her drawings also depict a world in which man's cruelty to man is limitless and unrelenting.

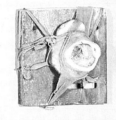

'Decorations' is a war memorial for peace. Ideally, she would like to see this work hung in a side-chapel or ante-chamber intended for use specifically for prayer or positive thinking against war. The memorial consists of ten plaques of rough-cut wood, each plaque measuring 6 × 11in (16 × 28cm) and hung at a distance of 4¼in (11cm) from the next. Each plaque represents a life sacrificed and supports a single bleached bone held in place by nails and strips of fabric bandage. The bandage is stretched taut and interlaced, using a variety of knotting and holding stitches, mainly detached chain, detached button-hole and coral stitch. The stress is taken by the bandage stitching. A campaign medal ribbon decoration is placed at the lower right corner of each plaque.

Rozanne's work does not suggest any connection with the world of fashion design, but nonetheless it was at the Royal College of Art's School of Fashion Design in London that she received her training. She followed this with a postgraduate course in textiles at Goldsmiths' College, London.

ASPECTS OF SHRUBSWOOD

LUCY GOFFIN

Lucy Goffin works with a view of Newhaven harbour. Beyond her studio window a sea of masts moves against the changing sky and bright fishing boats and ferries come and go. Beyond the harbour the hills are patterned by the seasons; bright yellow fields of rape in summer contrasted with the vivid green of young wheat, scarified chalky-brown earth after harvest. All this movement and change is reflected in her work.

'Aspects of Shrubswood' celebrates a garden which belonged to Bridget D'Oyley Carte. This garden in the Chilterns was the setting for many happy summer holidays during Lucy's childhood. Along with another piece, 'Kite Collage', it marks the beginning of a new development in her output. 'Kite Collage' was a commissioned piece and it was while working on this that Lucy came upon the work of the painter Harry Thuberon. She was greatly struck by the free, fluid quality of his work and resolved to capture the same freedom and fluidity using cloth and stitch. For some time she had been striving to establish a method of working which would free her from the necessity to turn over the edges of her cloth and she began now to stitch down the pieces with her machine. Using a series of different coloured threads she stitched down the rough-cut pieces with runs of stitches placed at close intervals. What emerged proved unexpected. Depths appeared which owed their being entirely to the effect the different coloured threads had upon their ground. She had found her 'canvas'.

Lucy Goffin was not trained as an embroiderer. She completed a diploma in ceramics at Harrow College of Art in 1970 and, in that same year, moved to Acheres in France to work with the Australian potter Gwyn Hansen.

Her involvement with textiles was brought about by a curious complexity of influences. First, her mother, who died when Lucy was only sixteen, had always made clothes and dolls for her two daughters and at the end of her life, when she was left partially paralysed by a series of strokes, she began to make simple collages with cut-out paper shapes. Secondly, her father was a designer with the D'Oyley Carte Opera Company. These combined influences conspired to move Lucy in the direction of theatrical design work and, on completing her training as a potter, she began to work for a ballet company, making costumes. Here she came under the influence of an individual who, like her mother, emphasised the importance of meticulous cutting and attention to detail and finishing. It was a rigorous, tough training.

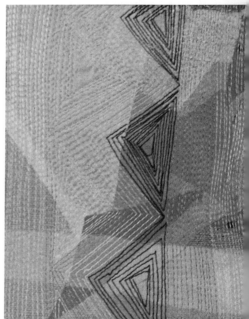

In the mid-Seventies Lucy began to produce a series of unique garments which, when not being worn, could serve as wall-pieces. These, coupled with ravishing little boxes and 'hats', formed the substance of her first exhibitions. Particularly memorable is a two-person exhibition she shared with the potter Mo Jupp at the British Crafts Centre in 1973.

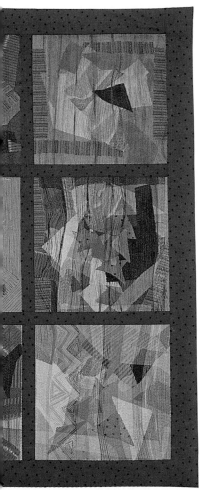

Thereafter, her work was included in many exhibitions in the United Kingdom, Japan, the USA, Switzerland and France, and over the years she has executed a number of interesting commissions including a coat-of-arms for the Banqueting House in Whitehall, London, and a large screen for the central window of the new Chester District Library. Since 1981 she has worked on the production of embroidery design for the annual spring and autumn collections of Jean Muir.

Lucy Goffin has served on the Crafts Council's Selection Committee and has lectured in textiles at West Surrey College of Art since 1979.

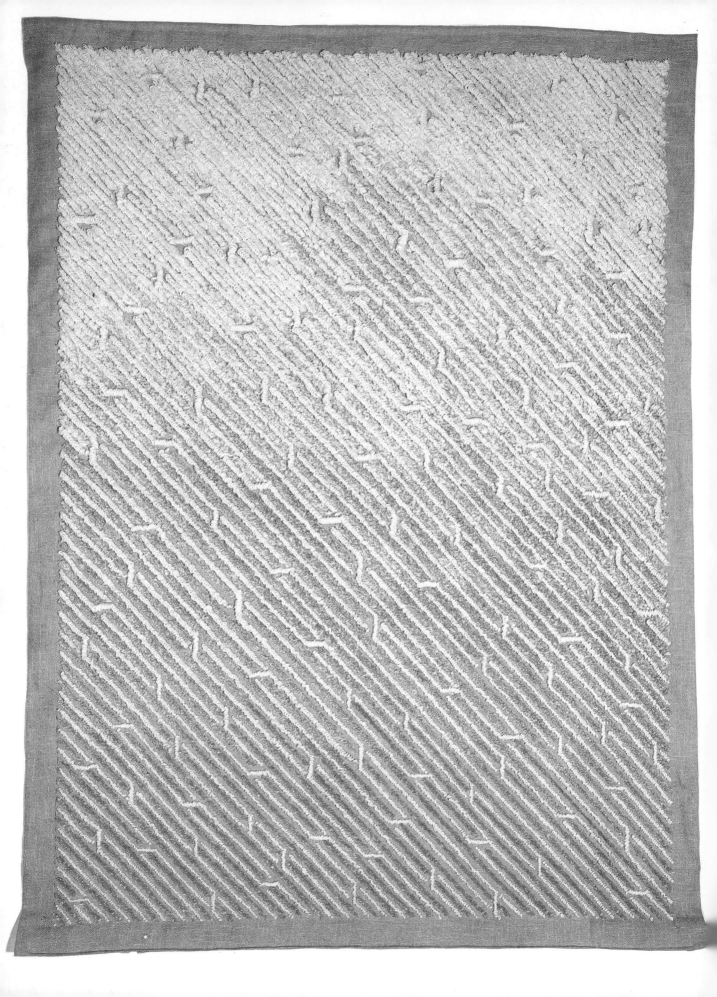

Spring Snowfall

JENNIFER HEX

'Spring Snowfall' was one of a series of pieces Jennifer Hex completed using lines of looped stitches with variations and with the inclusion of another element being a feature. In the case of 'Spring Thaw' this took the form of tufts. Her work is entirely hand-sewn.

Jennifer Hex completed a diploma in art in printmaking at the Glasgow School of Art in 1960 and spent the following year studying at Jordanhill College of Education, Glasgow. Since leaving college she has taught in various secondary schools and worked as a freelance embroiderer and as a part-time weaver. Her work is included in the Scottish Craft Collection.

Kimono

ROBIN GIDDINGS

Robin Giddings maintains that his aim is 'to create a wholly personal textile surface using the sewing-machine to replace the warp and allowing the flowing machine line to combine elements of a precious nature into web-like structures'.

'Kimono' is a fine example of the guipure lace techniques he employs. He used an 'Irish' Singer sewing-machine to produce the piece, adding some work on the Cornely machine. His preference for formal or clearly defined shapes is beautifully demonstrated in the delicate skeletal but sumptuously coloured kimono. Here the simplicity of form serves as an understatement to the extraordinary brilliance of colour and complex web-like structure of the fabric.

Robin Giddings completed a BA(Hons) in embroidery at Goldsmiths' College, London, in 1979 and an MA (with distinction) in textiles (guipure lace) at Manchester Polytechnic in 1980. In 1980 he joined the '62 Group.

He has work in the Museum of Modern Art, Kyoto, Japan, and in the Embroiderers' Guild collection at Hampton Court, and has exhibited widely in the UK and abroad.

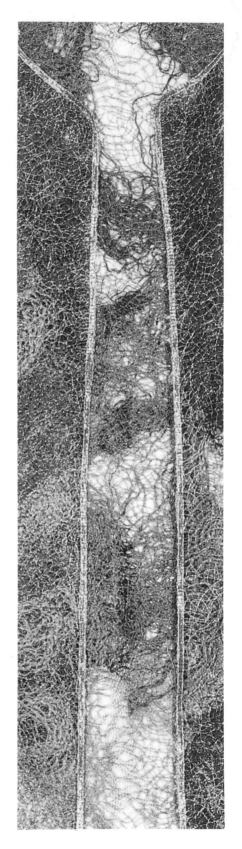

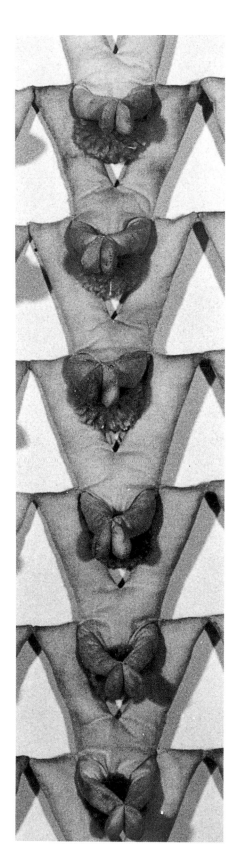

UPSIDEDOWN

CLAIRE JOHNSON

Claire Johnson looks at the world with a distinctly humorous eye. 'My work usually pokes fun at some element of human behaviour,' she explains.

In 'Upsidedown' she has attempted to convey an upside-down world, 'the sort of world children see when they hang from trees or bars in games, seeing how the view changes'.

Claire has written about the 'conception' of the small, three-dimensional figures which typify her work. She first began to work this way in her third year at Manchester Polytechnic, struggling to find an idiom through which to express her personal view of man's relationship with his environment. She claims that the first figures were crude and were created initially out of bought coloured fabrics and that subsequently they became 'horrific green knitted ones which have never been displayed'. Gradually, the small hand-dyed figures emerged, their delicate colours inspired by clover flowers which, she feels, exemplify man's link with nature and the vital balance maintained in the agricultural environment.

She made a series of figures with poppers stitched to their hands enabling them to grasp each other or their own limbs. She explored 'Jack-in-the-box' possibilities, inside-out boxes, pop-up and pop-out playing cards, using quilting and padding techniques and employing stitches such as plush stitch to further emphasise the softness of the fabric.

She rarely uses machine-embroidery because she wishes to avoid flattening the quilting and quilting is her favourite technique. She finds that it lends depth to a textile resulting in shadow effects which enhance the drama she seeks to exploit. She limits her 'stitching' to bullion and French knots, plush, stab and running stitches.

The subtle colour quality in her work is achieved by hand-dyeing with a paintbrush which enables the colours to merge and provides the possibility of using strong dramatic blocks or lines of colour.

Claire Johson completed a BA in creative embroidery at Manchester Polytechnic in 1983. She has been a member of the '62 Group since 1981, exhibiting in all their exhibitions in the UK and Japan and was one of the twelve British embroiderers featured in Diana Springall's book of that name.

Jays

NICOLA HENLEY

Nicola Henley owns to an obsession with birds. For the past few years since she graduated from Goldsmiths' College, London, with First Class Honours in embroidery and textiles in 1984, she has pursued this subject in all her work.

In January 1986 she was awarded a Crafts Council 'setting up' and maintenance grant and this enabled her to complete the conversion of an unusual Queen Anne gazebo in Bristol into a silk-screen workshop for fabric printing with discharge pigments. 'The Gazebo' stands in a rambling, walled garden visited by a large variety of birds, but, whenever possible, Nicola extends her bird-watching activities to the countryside, drawing at Chew Valley Lake, Bridgwater Bay, in the Peak District, and in parts of South Wales and on the south coast of Devon.

Birds, and in particular bird flight and spatial, aerial patterns have inspired her consistently for the past few years and she is interested in the way birds move within an environment. She tries to catch the characteristic flight patterns or movements as they relate to the ground, water or particular habitat.

In 'Jays' she has tried to describe the frantic, covert activities of this woodland bird because only glimpses of its unusual colours can be seen through the trees when they are observed and recorded. The piece also makes reference to the peculiar habit that jays have of burying acorns in the ground. The right-hand section is heavily machine-embroidered using torn up pieces of muslin which had previously been dyed and printed with tree-like images. Other materials – lace and paper, for example – were incorporated. The larger left section is dyed and printed with silk-screen images using discharge and direct printing as well as some hand-printing. Certain areas have been worked into with hand-embroidery, mainly running stitch, French knotting and other improvised marks.

TURBARY II

JANET LEDSHAM

Janet Ledsham trained as a painter. She is, at present, lecturer in embroidery at the University of Ulster, Belfast, and during the summer vacations she works in the marsh and moorland landscape of Northern Ireland, taking photographs, making drawings and gathering materials to be used in the construction of her pieces. She is especially intrigued by the peat cuttings which are a distinctive feature of the particular west coast landscape where she spends her holidays, the chevron patterns made by the spade during the process of peat cutting, and the effects made by the subsequent weathering of the exposed surfaces.

Small-scale work is frequently executed on location, using hand-stitching in order to create a spontaneous authentic interpretation, but when constructing the larger pieces she works largely from her photographic studies, using layers of linen which are slashed and hand-stitched together with quilting knots and seeding stitches.

She dyes her own fleeces and uses hand-made felt as a base and into this substructure she incorporates the dried materials collected from the landscape – mosses, heather and Equisetum, or 'horsetails' as they are commonly known. The pieces are then freely machined, hand-stitched and stiffened with sheets of adhesive and finally cut, folded and restructured.

Janet Ledsham has been a member of the '62 Group since 1980 and has exhibited in all the group exhibitions in the United Kingdom, in Europe and in Japan. Her work was included in the 1984 fifth international biennial of miniature textiles in Hungary and in the 1984 international exhibition of miniature textiles in Strasbourg, which also went on tour in Europe. In 1985 she was a participant in *9 Artists des Mini-textiles de Strasbourg* at La Filothèque DMC in Paris.

Recently, her work has been influenced by trips to Greece and Morocco and she has begun to experiment with hand-made papers.

EVE FALLING FROM GRACE

ALICE KETTLE

Alice Kettle's training as a painter reveals itself in an intuitive way of working and in a brilliant use of colour in her work. While it is difficult to point to the influence of any contemporary textile art in her work it is readily possible to trace the source of some of her iconography to the work of painters such as Klimt and Hundertwasser.

'Eve Falling from Grace' was worked using machine-embroidery over the entire surface. Alice modestly declares that, as she came to embroidery only relatively recently, she knows comparatively little about embroidery techniques. She claims that she uses what seem the quickest and most 'painterly' methods to express a circumstance.

She explained that the 'Eve' piece is like a waterfall, tumbling out of the wall onto the floor, so that the tapestry and carpet formats converge. Eve falls through the space into a worldly state. She is serpent-like and seductively beautiful, a state to which perhaps we all aspire.

Alice is concerned to break away from the customary two-dimensional format of embroidery and often moulds and manipulates figures out of the surface of the piece. She has turned to embroidery quite deliberately in an attempt to embrace a medium which has been traditionally the province of women and the deliberate act of turning her back on painting as a vehicle for her work is motivated by the conviction that painting is a male-dominated art form. All of this might create an impression of a somewhat aggressive individual, but that would be extremely misleading, for Alice Kettle is essentially a gentle person, quiet of voice and full of delicate sensibilities. If one bears in mind that she was reared in the wholly male-orientated world of Winchester College where her father has taught for many years, it is not surprising that she feels called upon to assert her femininity. She uses embroidery as well as the female form in recognition of her own deep roots in a traditionally female medium. The women in her pieces very much reflect her own circumstances. She tries to let the fabric create its own form and dimension, sewing to great intensity, never using a hoop, but always working with a machine. In certain areas she moulds and manipulates the fabric in a more controlled way.

Alice Kettle gained a BA in fine art in 1984 from the University of Reading and completed a postgraduate diploma in textile art at Goldsmiths' College, London, in 1986. She has returned to live and work in Winchester, sharing work space in the design workshops of Winchester School of Art.

REFLECTIONS II

MOYRA McNEILL

When planning 'Reflections', Moyra McNeill had two controlling factors in mind. One, that the work should be based on a subject that she 'knew' and the other that it should be worked with a view to it receiving hard wear.

Bearing in mind that the declared aim of the Embroiderers' Guild exhibition was to attract architects, it is particularly apt that the shapes reflected in glass-clad tower blocks should provide the subject for this piece, although Moyra points out that she had already begun a series of pieces based on architectural subjects before the brief was delivered. This subject appealed to her because she feels that the reflected shapes 'lend a liquidity to what is otherwise a relentlessly rigid form'. She is fascinated by the fact that the 'moving distorted shapes dominate the structure rather than the reverse'.

She based the piece on a traditional ground of canvas and worked the frame of the windows formally on the grain. The remainder of the piece was stitched freely and diagonally in order to interpret the moving quality of the reflections. The threads employed are a mixture of synthetic and natural fibres and very long stitches are held in place with a machine zig-zag.

Moyra McNeill's publications, *Blackwork Embroidery, Pulled Thread, Quilting* and *Machine Embroidery, Lace and See-through Techniques* are well known and she has had many articles published in *Embroidery* magazine.

Bayeux 1984

JEAN LITTLEJOHN

Jean Littlejohn has lived in and around Maidenhead, Berkshire, most of her life. She works at Windsor and Maidenhead College of Fine Art as joint lecturer with her friend and colleague Jan Beaney, teaching City and Guilds students.

Holidays with her husband and young daughter are spent most frequently in France – in Normandy and Brittany – and it is an on-going love affair with the atmospheres and architecture of France that has fostered a series of pieces of which 'Bayeux' is one.

France is a country of contradictions, Jean claims. She is intrigued by the fact that while the landscape is very organised – fields of sunflowers, fields of corn, straight rows of poplars testifying to the orderly, pragmatic nature of the French – the buildings, in contrast, often appear to be crumbling.

Her theory is that there is, as might be expected, a totally practical explanation for this state of affairs. If buildings are maintained in a pristine condition, rates immediately escalate. It might well be true – better to leave the façades to crumble while shoring up the interiors! In any event, the result is a curious juxtaposition of neatness and chaos, suggesting the essential schizophrenia of the French. Jean loves the fact that they can never resist 'dressing' a building. Even when it seems to be collapsing, you can always find a window-box stuffed with flowers.

In making these pieces, which reflect the dreamlike, mysterious atmospheres that she associates with her holidays in Normandy and Brittany, Jean works on a background of felt. She blends several fabrics together – muslin, scrim, calico, lace – stitching them onto the background, using both machine- and hand-stitching to emphasise or reinforce the forms. Her aim is to create a fabric out of which the images grow, not to present a surface on which forms have been superimposed. She likes understatement, but accepts that it is often achieved only with a good deal of effort. 'I like the swan paradox,' she says. 'All serenity on the surface and paddling like hell underneath!'

Once the fabrics have been stitched into place she treats the surface with dyes, spraying or sponging them on.

The quality of light in France is something she attempts to capture in this way – something Monet knew a great deal about when painting those crumbling façades – the fragmentary, ephemeral quality so difficult to encapsulate in paint or thread.

78

Byzantine I

Polly Moore

'Byzantine I' was the first of a series based on recent research that Polly Moore has carried out into Byzantine art. Her interest in mosaics was aroused originally by a floor she saw at Fishbourne, Chichester. The crumbling and disintegrating qualities of this mosaic with its layer upon layer of patterns attracted her attention and led to a study of Byzantine mosaics. In these she found the muted palette of the Romans replaced by strong vibrant colours: purples, maroons, browns and rusts contrasted with areas of patinated bronze, copper and gold.

In the early design stages she intended to work around a series of simple shapes which repeatedly occur in the borders of Byzantine paintings, but later she modified the final panel to concentrate on an exploration and manipulation of the colour combined with the patina of precious metals, while still retaining the feeling of a mosaic.

Polly Moore completed a BA in textile and fashion at Loughborough College in 1976 and went on to do an Art Teacher's Certificate at Leeds Polytechnic in 1977. Since leaving college she has taught in a variety of schools and institutes and since 1981 has been a lecturer at the London College of Fashion.

Edge Lane

JANE McKEATING

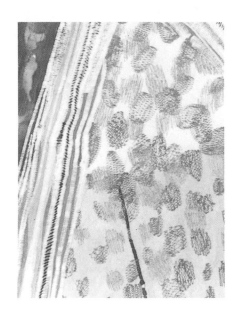

In 1986 Jane McKeating lived in Chorlton cum Hardy, and she named the piece illustrated here after the lane in which her home was situated. The work gradually evolved from initial drawings. Returning home from a shopping trip one day, she found the carrier bags blocking the doorway behind her and she felt as if she was encapsulated in a space dominated by a window whose mass of overhanging plants seemed to infect the entire atmosphere of the room. It seemed as though she could water the very air and make it grow. Much cutting and layering, stitching and dyeing resulted in the final piece which attempts to recall the freshness of that summer day deep inside a city.

Jane McKeating completed a BA(Hons) in embroidery and textiles at Goldsmiths' College, London, in 1983 and went on to achieve an MA with distinction at Manchester Polytechnic in 1984. During 1985 she was artist in residence at Malbank School, Nantwich.

FISH IN FLIGHT

JACQUELINE MURRANT

'Fish in Flight' was made in a spirit of defiance. Jacqueline Murrant took great pleasure in making something that has no great meaning behind it. She simply enjoyed using her favourite colours and producing a beautiful and decorative piece. The idea of the fish came from a mosaic she saw while travelling in Spain, the shape of the creature having a particular appeal. The piece was created purely for pleasure and Jacqueline hopes that others will enjoy it as well.

'Fish in Flight' was made up of 99 per cent silk, hand-dyed by Jacqueline herself, and was put together employing traditional pieced quilting methods.

Jacqueline Murrant was trained at Cleveland College of Art and Design and Goldsmiths' College, London, where she attained a BA(Hons) in textiles. In 1985 she became a member of Quilt Art.

THE LUNCH PARTY

BETTY MYERSCOUGH

Betty Myerscough's work is mainly the result of her observations of life — especially of people and their surroundings. She particularly enjoys capturing a moment in time. 'The Lunch Party' is a fine example of this genre. Looking down from her studio window one warm summer day she liked the view of a business lunch in progress. Recording it at the time with a quick sketch and notes, she later developed it into a large hanging with hand-painting and machine-embroidery.

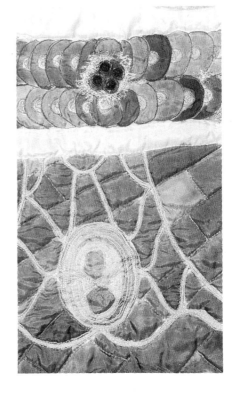

Betty Myerscough studied at the Glasgow School of Art from 1950 to 1953 and completed a postgraduate diploma in 1955. On leaving college she worked as a designer for P. Coates Ltd in Glasgow and in 1959 became a full-time lecturer in charge of embroidery at Gray's School of Art.

When she married she was obliged to move south and from 1961 to 1963 she worked as a part-time lecturer at Canterbury College of Art. While bringing up her family she worked as a freelance designer, selling her work through exhibitions, working to commission and writing articles on embroidery for magazines. Since 1973 she has been a part-time lecturer at the Chelsea School of Art, London, and has continued to work as a freelance textile artist.

She has executed many commissions and exhibited her work widely both in Britain and abroad.

THREE OF A KIND –
SUMMER/AUTUMN/WINTER

HERTA PULS

Over the years Herta Puls has developed a particular interest in the tribal embroideries of Central America, India and Thailand and has had a number of books and articles on these subjects published as well as lecturing on them. She has travelled widely in quest of source material. Some of the techniques she has explored during her researches into ethnic textiles have influenced her own work.

Of 'Three of a Kind' she explained that it started with drawings of landscape and fences in Gloucestershire. Fences gave her the feature around and through which she could express the mood and her feeling for different seasons: large monochrome areas of fields, abundance of colour in summer, glistening ice and snow in winter. The icy-looking fields were, in fact, polythene-covered hillsides of potato culture in Jersey.

The most profound influence on her working techniques, apart from hand- and machine-embroidery, has been Mola art, the unique way of using space and vibrant colour with a multi-layered appliqué technique which she learned from the Kuma Indians of Panama.

She prefers hand- to machine-embroidery, the slower working process allowing more time for thinking, consideration and reappraisal.

Herta Puls came to England from Hamburg in 1939 and was introduced to embroidery by Constance Howard. She completed the City and Guilds Certificate in embroidery, and also studied at Newport College of Art, West of England College of Art, Bristol, and the London College of Fashion.

THE MIRROR

PADDY RAMSAY

Paddy is like a humming-bird, tiny, vivid, startling. She has a direct northern way of 'spilling the beans', allowing glimpses into a personal world which provides the source of all her work. Looking back at earlier pieces one concludes that there are two central characters – Paddy herself and her black cat, Mici. She has been quoted frequently as saying that all her stitched work is an extension of her drawing, that she uses her sewing-machine as a paintbrush, her threads as her palette and her fabrics as her canvas, but what has not been said, perhaps, is that each piece forms, as it were, a chapter in a continuing autobiography, albeit the images sometimes posing a riddle which may be deciphered only if one has a 'key'.

Of 'The Mirror', Paddy offers a direct explanation:

> The embroidery is the culmination of a piece I had been going to do called 'The Thistle and the Rose'. It was to have been of the life of my ex-husband and myself. I never did it. I was doing the drawings for it when he left me. It was to have been of us sitting working in front of the fire with stained-glass windows depicting various scenes from our past in the background. Over the fireplace was a mirror that was supposed to reflect our future. I never knew what to put in it. I have always had a psychic streak. Obviously – no future together! So this piece is called 'The Mirror'. It is the future. I sit working with all my inspirational things round me and the clock at 7.30pm and *EastEnders* on the TV and headphones round my neck so I can plug into either the TV or the stereo and the ever present Mici. The white roses are, of course, me – the white rose of Yorkshire. I like the symbolism of flowers: rhododendrons mean danger, ivy means fidelity. It is a highly personal piece, as most of my recent wall-hung things have been over the past two turbulent years.

Of the technicalities she explained that she draws with the sewing-machine needle and then colours in.

Paddy Ramsay completed a BA(Hons) in textiles and embroidery at Birmingham Polytechnic in 1971. Subsequently she worked in haute couture both in London and Canada. She returned to England in 1981 and now lives in Jesmond, Newcastle-upon-Tyne.

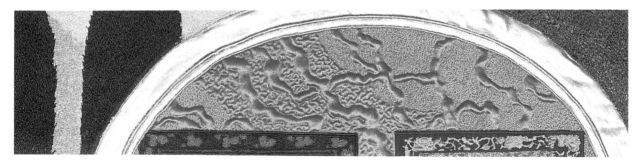

UNTITLED WALLHANGING

SUE RANGELEY

The piece illustrated here is typical of the very distinctive style that has come to be associated with Sue Rangeley's name, involving quilting techniques and hand- and machine-stitching. The pale, porcellanous colours, the delicately moulded scallop shells and the subtle air-brushed and hand-painted motifs are quintessentially 'Rangeley'.

Sue explains that in this piece the mood of her colour palette was related to fragments of frescoes and early Italian carvings that caught her imagination, their incised and carved textures translated here into quilting. As with much of her output this piece is conceived as part of an overall scheme and will form a centrepiece in a design plan that may incorporate such elements as hand-stencilling and rag-rolling of walls and wood surfaces.

Sue Rangeley was trained as a painter, completing a diploma in art and design in fine art and painting at Lancaster Polytechnic in 1970. In 1975 she set up a studio in Stow-on-the-Wold, Gloucestershire, and commenced working professionally in textiles. Later she moved to her present home in Charlbury, Oxfordshire.

Sue has executed many private commissions for painted and quilted textiles and the range of her output covers painted and embroidered quilts, screens, curtains and cushions, mainly in silk fabrics; fine silk and wool canvas work for cushions and carpets, integrating metallic threads; silk appliqué and fashion textiles, including one-off evening and bridal wear involving rich, decorative embroidery, bead-work and spray-dyeing; and hand-painting on silk.

This type of work is necessarily very labour intensive and Sue has gradually given up her regular teaching commitments, with the exception of occasional courses or blocks of teaching, in order to concentrate on the production of individual pieces.

Her work is included in the Embroiderers' Guild collection at Hampton Court and in the Cheltenham and Gateshead museums and art galleries and has been widely exhibited in the United Kingdom, the USA and in France and Australia.

CROWS

EIRIAN SHORT

Eirian Short was born in Pembrokeshire and, after teaching at Goldsmiths' College, London, from 1954 to 1985, she returned to live in Wales. Since 1978 her work has been based almost entirely on aspects of the Pembrokeshire landscape.

Rocky outcrops are one of the dominant features of this landscape and, from her studio window, she looks out on to a particularly spectacular example of this phenomenon. She has used this dramatic rock formation in several recent pieces but crows have emerged as the central preoccupation. For Eirian, the most dominant living things in the landscape are the crows and rooks which regularly mob the buzzards and drive them off. They are active outside her window all day and, as she sits stitching, the shadow cast by a passing crow often falls across her work. In 'Garn Meibion Owen' they were merely incidental details, but the latest piece has become virtually nine crow 'portraits'. The landscape in the centre is another view of Garn Meibion Owen.

Eirian works in one of two techniques: either entirely in French knots, giving a pointillist effect of dots of colour closely juxtaposed, or in straight stitches, making marks which are the equivalent of a painter's brush-strokes. She tries to sum up the mood and atmosphere of a place and give the viewer the feeling that they could 'walk into the picture'.

Asked about her method of working, she states that she begins by making a fairly quick drawing on the spot and takes colour photographs and slides. Back in the studio, using all three, she works out the composition of the landscape and draws it to full size. She usually has a feeling of what is the 'right' size for a particular piece. At this stage she usually needs to return to the site as she finds that there is rarely enough information in her first quick drawing. Photographs are inadequate, too, she feels, as they fail to convey sufficient information about space and form.

She makes corrections on the full-scale drawing and also adds verbal notes in the manner of Edward Lear. The main lines of the corrected drawing are then traced onto the base fabric with embroidery carbon and the main areas of colour filled in in long, straight stitches, much as a painter tones a canvas. She prefers to put in the lightest and darkest areas first, to establish the tonal range. It is then a matter of painstakingly building up the detail, layer by layer, which, in the case of 'Crows', took eight months.

Eirian finds it difficult to remember exactly how the design for 'Crows' evolved. She remembers having a feeling that the birds were too important to be just incidental to the landscape. The practical difficulties of working on a stretched fabric 5ft (1.5m) square encouraged her towards the idea of making the panel in nine sections with eight of them containing crow 'portraits'. She worked in Appleton's crewel wools on Welsh flannel. In these

wools each colour comes in a range of seven or more tones, giving the stitcher an approximation to a painter's palette. A single thread can be used for very fine detail and colours can be mixed in the needle to give a lively broken surface. Welsh flannel makes a perfect base to work on, being strong but soft and enhancing the sensuous pleasure of stitching.

She rarely feels that a piece is finished, but when a deadline arrives she accepts that she must stop at that point and show the work as it is.

UNTITLED

MARY SPYROU

Despite the fact that her life has been spent largely in Britain, Mary Spyrou's work reveals her Cypriot origin. Something in the vivid colours and images she employs speaks of warmth and the sun. Her personality, too, has an openness not usually found in the British temperament.

In 1986 the Crafts Council awarded her a travelling grant and Mary fulfilled a long-standing ambition to visit Egypt. She discovered, as travellers so frequently do, that the reality was at variance with her anticipations. She had hoped to find a wealth of interesting textiles in a living tradition, to be able to study ethnic techniques and to draw upon an available source of information. She was disappointed in these hopes. Apart from excellent museum collections she found that the chief benefit of the trip was in the actual contact with physical Egypt. The light, the colours, the juxtaposition of the grand and the decaying, the visual paradoxes, these were the things that brought her work alive.

In order to illustrate this point, characteristically to herself as much as to the onlooker, she has placed two pieces side by side on her studio wall. One is a vivid, sapphire-coloured piece, the other a piece she completed while at the Royal College of Art, executed in ochre colours. The message is immediately clear. The textures and colours of the sapphire piece leap and sing in the chilly room, while, despite its undeniably fine qualities, the other piece seems dull and muted in contrast.

Currently, Mary is writing an educational book, focussing on ethnic techniques. She is not particularly forthcoming about her own way of working, feeling that an informed look at any one of her pieces will reveal the methods employed. What she admits to is a great interest in surface decoration. Her work is influenced by decorative mosaics, Islamic ceramics, Khelim design and most particularly by her love of Coptic arts. The Coptic museum in Cairo excited her more than anything she saw in her travels. The pieces illustrated here and on the back of the jacket were largely generated by this encounter and, if one is to judge them by their larger, freer, more vivid quality, it was a catalytic one.

Mary Spyrou was educated in Britain, completing her BA in textiles at Trent Polytechnic in 1981 and going on to the Royal College of Art's Tapestry Department in London, from which she emerged in 1984 with an MA in textile design. Since leaving college she has been teaching, dividing her time between working with Asian women at the Whitechapel Asian Studies Centre, with mentally handicapped adults at the City and East College, London, and teaching at Downsview School.

SAINT PAUL PUBLIC LIBRARY

JAN 23 1997

DATE DUE

Materials are due before
closing on date stamped

*TO RENEW LIBRARY MATERIAL
BY TOUCH TONE PHONE, CALL
292-6002 ON OR BEFORE THE DUE
DATE.*

OVERDUE FINES
Adult material: 25¢ per day per item
Juvenile material: 5¢ per day per item

*A computer generated phone call will
alert you when your item becomes
7 days overdue. This phone notice
replaces the mail notice.*

WALLHANGING TRIANGLE I

JOANNE SATCHELL

Egyptian wall paintings have for some time been of particular interest to Joanne Satchell and she has combined this interest with another in tassels and braids to produce the piece entitled 'Wallhanging Triangle' in which the basic triangular motifs are derived from Elizabethan dress ornamentation and are shaded to draw the eye to the tassels. In this piece she has combined canvas work with appliqué and hand-made felt to produce a contrast between angularity and softness in the design.

The felt background is constructed in one piece. Coloured threads of silk and wool, together with small pieces of coloured felt are combined to create the desired colours and textures. Canvas work embroidered with silks is built up in layers of colour to give a softly graduated effect. The tassels are constructed from layered silks, cut to reveal each colour, giving a three-dimensional effect similar to that achieved in the canvas work.

Joanne Satchell studied at Loughborough College of Art and Design completing her BA(Hons) in textiles and fashion in 1983. Her work was included in the 1983 'Young Blood' exhibition at the Barbican, London, and in a two-woman exhibition at the Embroiderers' Guild, Hampton Court. In 1982 she had a three-weeks' industrial placement at the Nottingham Costume and Textile Museum. Currently she works as a contract designer with Carpets of Worth at Stourport-on-Severn where her work involves her in several skills, including computer-aided design.

ROTATING SPECTRUM INTERWOVEN

ANN SUTTON

Although her reputation as a textile artist has been established in the field of woven rather than stitched textiles, Ann Sutton was trained primarily as an embroiderer. A feeling that embroidery was essentially about 'decorating the surface' drove her to investigate weaving. Working within this discipline she was able to explore the underlying structures of fabric and, inevitably, because she has that type of enquiring and restless intelligence, she sought new ways of drawing attention to those elements which surprised and delighted her.

Either way the results have had many applications. She it was who first conceived the idea of the 'miniature textile' to counter the fashion so popular in the early Seventies of producing mega works of art whether in paint or textile and in consequence acted as catalyst to the series of international miniature textile exhibitions which followed.

During the period of her marriage to John Makepeace, the furniture designer-craftsman, she indulged in a brief sortie into the realm of furniture design, producing floorpads, chairs and 'loveseats' constructed from seamless knitted tubes.

Her work, in conjunction with the Welsh woollen industry, designing furnishing fabrics and a range of children's wear, is yet another illustration of the versatility of application of which she is capable. She even ventured into the area of 'small industry' when, in 1974 living near Banbury, she discovered that she could harness the forces of home-bound married women and successfully launched a village production workshop, producing rugs, bed-covers and hangings.

It is not surprising to discover that her latest preoccupation is a newly acquired home computer, offering the exciting prospect of computer-dictated design. Her approach has always been mathematical rather than 'romantic'. She seeks logical solutions to problems, but she is quick to point out, with a satisfied chuckle, that there are bonuses to be found even in this method of working.

The bonus in the piece 'Rotating Spectrum Interwoven', for example, proves to be the systematic juxtaposition of colours which occurs automatically. The piece was the first stitched work Ann Sutton had produced in a long time. After many years of woven structural work she found it interesting to come back to stitching. The bands of silk run right through the piece and do not start and stop at the intersections. Such details matter to her. The piece is designed to sit flat on the wall with no indication of how it retains its equilibrium.

Maintaining equilibrium is not one of Ann's problems. These days she lives in a beautifully converted house in the heart of Arundel, Sussex, near enough to the station to dispense with a car, London a mere hour's train-ride away. The white-painted clap-board walls find a logical response in vertical Venetian-type blinds on the windows. There is a noticeable paucity of the 'home-spun'. A black Aga stove dominates the kitchen. There is a logic in the arrangement of her spaces which does not disallow warmth, comfort and that essential element of surprise that is to be found wherever someone with a very particular eye puts things together. Here, one feels, is someone who knows how to live.

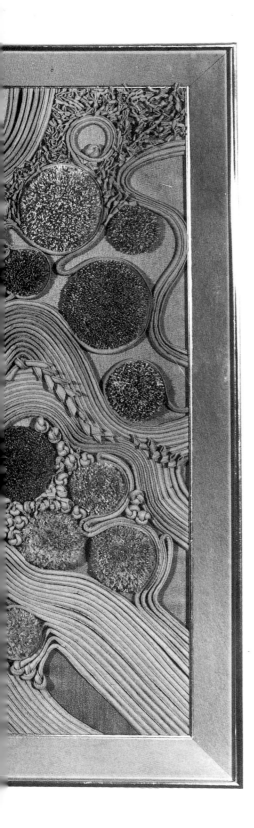

AUTUMN IN NARA

DIANA SPRINGALL

The pair of panels entitled 'Autumn in Nara' in low relief form part of a series of pieces based on Diana Springall's journeys to Japan and depict an Isuin garden. Images of the gardens have not been slavishly copied, however. Instead, the bare essence of her observations has been extracted. The work reveals only sensations of gentle colour, raked gravel, combed moss and meticulously clipped Sharenbai bushes. The technique employed to depict the scene is hand-tufting in wool, combined with piped felt. The components are hand-stitched onto a dupion ground.

Diana Springall was trained at Goldsmiths' College, London, and has a National Diploma in Design in painting, an Art Teacher's Training Certificate, a London University diploma in the history of art and City and Guilds embroidery qualification. She was principal lecturer in art at Stockwell College of Education for eleven years until 1980 and served as external examiner to the universities of Bath and Birmingham.

She has been a life-member of the Embroiderers' Guild for over twenty years and served as the guild's chairman from 1978 to 1985. She has always worked diligently to promote British embroidery both in the United Kingdom and abroad and has travelled widely, conducting lecture tours in the USA and Canada, visiting Mexico and the San Blas Islands to conduct research into embroidery.

In 1978 Diana Springall visited Japan with the World Crafts Council and in 1982 she organised the first exhibition of British contemporary and historical embroidery, giving lectures and workshops during her stay there. In 1985 she organised the second British embroidery exhibition to visit Osaka and Tokyo, entitled 'Twelve British Embroiderers', and was the author of the full-colour catalogue accompanying the exhibition. In 1986 she participated in the first international craft competition in Kyoto, Japan. Between 1984 and 1986 she paid three study visits to China.

Her publications include *Canvas Embroidery, Embroidery* (the 1980 BBC publication to accompany the series of the same name for which she acted as consultant) and *Twelve British Embroiderers*.

THE KITE FESTIVAL, JAIPUR

DOROTHY TUCKER

Dorothy Tucker's piece 'The Kite Festival, Jaipur', was bought by the architectural firm of Ahrends, Burton and Koralek and is destined to be hung in a hospital on the Isle of Wight.

In January 1984 Dorothy went to north-west India on a textile study tour and within fifteen minutes' walk from the hotel in Delhi where she stayed was the house where she had lived as a little girl. She found the noise, the colour, the light and air a totally familiar experience. The following two weeks or so were to be a profound mixture of experiences and emotions for her.

She arrived in Jaipur just before the kite festival. All the shops were trading briskly and men were coating miles of string stretched between posts and trees along the roadside with dyed glass powder. She and her husband bought two kites each and with these fragile diamond shapes of brightly coloured tissue paper held high, they wound their way through the crowded streets, attracting a good deal of attention.

Exhausted by the morning, she chose to stay in the hotel for a while and, sitting by an open window high up, she saw the city, sprawled out in the afternoon heat, all the noise and movement contained between the blocks of pink and turquoise buildings and kites wheeling quietly above. She was inspired to draw.

From all the photographs and textiles she brought home, it was around these drawings that bundles of cotton waste that she had picked up from workshop floors, photographs of buildings and postcards, even fragments of fabric and paper bags, began to gather. A collage emerged using paper, hand-made several years earlier.

Before going to India Dorothy Tucker had been exploring every variation of herringbone stitch (a stitch, incidentally, to be found on many Indian textiles) and the idea of working with one stitch. More recently she had become interested in felt-making and began to explore ways of combining stitch with felt until she was ready to begin her final piece. There were three major challenges to overcome: the scale, the need to achieve a textile piece which did not simply reproduce the collage but went beyond it to satisfy her sense of what embroidery is all about, and to achieve an Indian idea or 'feel' without incorporating traditional patterns.

The starting point for the piece was the time when Dorothy's senses were finely tuned and became emotionally fused with the light, colour, movement and sound, feel and smell held within the one place. The work evolved as she followed these feelings through drawings and collage, selecting fabrics and threads. Then followed a long search through various techniques and design ideas when she was preoccupied with questioning what embroidery is and should be in the contemporary world, until the piece finally emerged, complete.

Dorothy Tucker completed a diploma course in embroidery at Goldsmiths' College, London, in 1978. Since leaving college she has been involved continuously in teaching in a variety of situations including the Roehampton Institute; Ravensbourne, Marylebone, Paddington, and Blackheath Schools of Art; Digby Stuart College and the Eileen Leeky Health Clinic, Putney; and Barnet General Hospital.

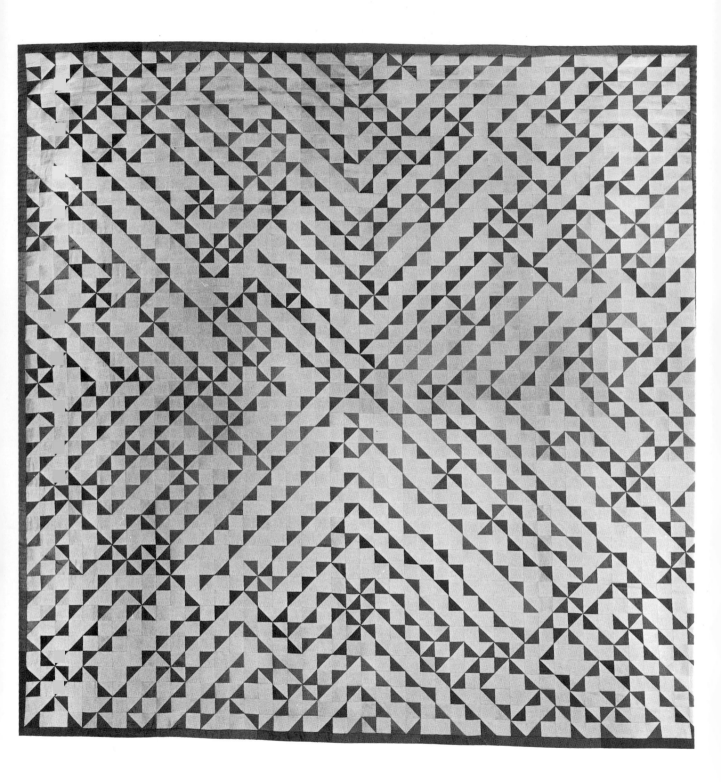

ILE JOYEUSE

VERONICA TOGNERI

'Ile Joyeuse' was completed in 1984. It is a hand-sewn patchwork quilt made of silk with cotton lining and padding. The piece was inspired by the summer colours and atmospheres of the Hebridean island where Veronica once lived. Like all her patchwork, it is hand-sewn and is composed of a few simple, geometric shapes which are allowed to grow in a cell-like manner to form an irregular all-over pattern. Having worked previously on a large scale with cotton, she turned in this piece to using silk for its clearer, more luminous colour.

Veronica Togneri received her diploma in embroidery and weaving from Glasgow School of Art and followed this with a post-diploma scholarship. In 1962 she set up her own studio and weaving workshop. Between 1983 and 1984 she was able to develop her work in silk patchwork with the aid of a Scottish Development Agency Craft Fellowship.

THERMAL

STEPHANIE TUCKWELL

Stephanie Tuckwell cannot say how textiles came to be her chosen medium, but remembers that as a little girl she did a great deal of sewing and that she has always enjoyed making clothes. Her work is largely intuitive, although drawings and photographs frequently provide the starting point for her pieces. She commences, customarily, with a number of cut-out shapes which are moved about and arranged and rearranged until a pattern emerges which satisfies her. The materials, silk and paper, are sprayed and painted with dye and acrylics, then stitched, plastered and glued into position. Sometimes portions are ripped off and then replaced. Very rarely does she have in mind a definite image; rather, the image declares itself. At one time she used only natural dyes, but declares that such purity no longer excites her.

Her present way of working came about when she decided to give up making soft furnishings because she felt she needed time to herself. It was a bold step and one that has paid off. The chalky surfaces and faded, subtle colours reveal her interest in frescoes, in tempera, in the work of such painters as Giotto and Piero della Francesca and in the sun-bleached, architectural shapes of Tuscany.

Stephanie Tuckwell studied textiles and embroidery at Goldsmiths' College, London, from 1972 to 1975. When she left college she was undecided about her future direction and followed a course of teacher training at Brighton. She was awarded a West Midlands Arts Craft fellowship in conjunction with the University of Aston, Birmingham, from 1976 to 1977 and in 1978 she set up a workshop in Rotherhithe, London. Here she made spray-dyed, embroidered, soft furnishings which she sold through Liberty's One-Off Department, Browns Living and the Craft Council's shop at the Victoria and Albert Museum, in London. In 1984 she had her first one-man show at the Oxford Gallery.

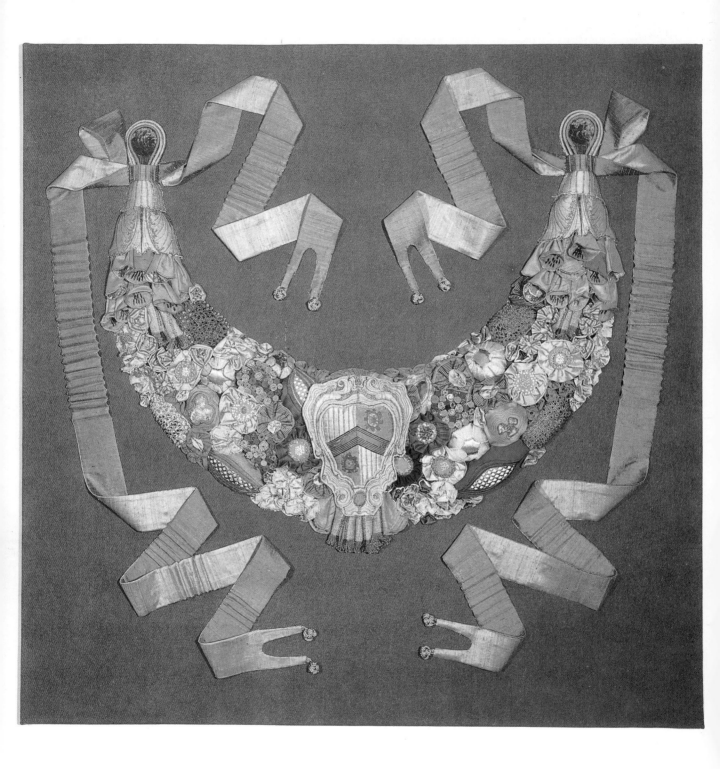

FESTOON

RUTH TUDOR

Ruth Tudor's three-dimensional work was born out of a dissatisfaction with the more traditional forms of embroidery she had previously employed. She came to feel that the pieces she produced were merely further experiments in texture, colour or technique and lacked completeness. She wished to produce something which went beyond mere embellishment and was, in itself, a complete statement.

Her first tentative statements in the new medium took the form of dolls and she learnt a great deal during the process of exploring this discipline. She used simple materials like calico and kapok and in some cases wired the forms to enable them to stand.

After two years of experimentation she discovered a book entitled *English Monumental Sculpture since the Renaissance*. Here she found a rich source of inspiration in the illustrations of altar tombs, mural tablets and elaborate memorials. She visited the sites of many of these memorials and began to study the period architecture and costume in greater depth. From all this research her own characteristic style emerged. At present these architectural details, effigies and sculptures continue to provide her with the main source of inspiration. In them she finds a source of rich decoration to interpret in fabric and thread.

'Festoon' was mounted on a background with the intention of making it more durable and easy to handle, but normally her three-dimensional work is mounted over pieces of machine ply cut to the shape of the pieces. The individual flowers for the swag were made in a variety of materials using both machine- and hand-stitching and were then mounted onto a padded shape on a slat frame.

ARCADIAN SUMMER

VERINA WARREN

Verina Warren's work has always been based on English landscapes, seascapes and gardens and the two panels entitled 'Arcadian Summer' are no exception, although the scale employed is larger than that normally associated with her work. The panels depict the transition of the cultivated garden into the wild, from formal flowers in pots to the magical wild garden and ultimately to the open meadow. Although each panel retains an identity, the interchange of colour gives continuity by allowing the eye to move easily from one to the other. The distant seascape gives a suggested, continuous horizon line, adding further continuity to the design, and the expanse of sea and sky in the meadow panel gives spatial contrast to the textural surfaces.

Heavy-weight silk was used as a background in the panels. The colour was air-brushed and hand-painted onto the fabric, using silk dyes. Machine-embroidery, whip stitch and exaggerated whip was worked over the surface, colour being used intuitively as the work progressed. The application of the technique was used very freely and although texture is used abundantly, it never totally obscures the background. The painted surfaces have been allowed to show through the embroidery to lend added depth.

The outer bands of mounting board were air-brushed with acrylic paints to open out, yet enclose, the embroidered sections. Silk-wrapped borders were inserted to enhance the shading on the card mount and also to pick up and reflect the light. The green moulding was chosen not only for its colour matching but because it helped to take the design to the outer perimeters, thereby 'opening up' the embroidery.

Verina Warren was born in Durham and graduated from Goldsmiths' College, London with a diploma in art and design in 1968. She taught, at first in a part-time and later in a full-time capacity, until 1973 when she went freelance. By this time she had developed her unique way of combining embroidery and painting and established a partnership with her husband who deals with the assembly and finishing of her work and acts as her business manager and administrator. In 1986 her very successful book *Landscape in Embroidery* was published.

Verina has work in the following public collections: The Victoria and Albert Museum, London; The Museum of Modern Art, Kyoto, Japan; The National Gallery of Victoria, Australia; the Leeds City Council, Lincoln and Humberside Arts and East Midlands Arts Collections and the Embroiderers' Guild Collection, Hampton Court.

SILK HANGING

KATHERINE VIRGILS

Katherine Virgils uses paper, paint, metal, wood, wire, gesso and cloth to record her feelings about objects she likes. She states that she is interested in the tension that exists between structure and chaos. Her work reflects a preoccupation with the effect of decay upon surfaces. 'In a way my pictures are portraits of physical processes – breaking down the accepted order, stretching materials to their limit,' she explains.

She admires the work of Turner above all else and has been influenced by subjects as diverse as baroque architecture, Arapaho and Cree artefacts, Plains Indian buffalo hides, icons, surrealism and Egyptian wall paintings.

The stitched silk hanging illustrated here is one of a series made in 1986.

Katherine Virgils was born in Houston, Texas, USA. She chose to study in Britain as she was convinced of the excellence of British schools of art and, having accomplished her BA with First Class Honours in painting at Ravensbourne College of Art in 1979, she went on to do an MA in tapestry at the Royal College of Art, London, completing her studies in 1981.

Her brother was studying in Italy and, as her parents were in the Far East, she frequently visited him there rather than returning to the United States. Italy and Italian architecture in particular were to have a profound influence on the development of her work.

In 1982 she received a setting up grant from the Crafts Council and was able to establish a studio in London.

Her work has been exhibited widely in Britain, West Germany, Switzerland, Austria and the USA and she has had one-person exhibitions at the Camden Arts Centre and at the Thumb Gallery, London. Her work is included in the collections of the Crafts Council, the Sainsbury Collection, Norwich, and has been bought by the Contemporary Art Society. In 1985 Katherine Virgils was chosen by Lady Sainsbury to be the recipient of the Paul Reilly Award at the Chelsea Crafts Fair.

TADDINGTON MOOR

KATE WELLS

A recurring theme in all the work of Kate Wells is the English landscape. 'Taddington Moor' was executed during the summer and autumn of 1986. In subject matter and technique it is a natural progression from recent works in which wide expanses of rural landscape are considered for their spatial and textural detail by a process of freely painting on canvas and then over-working in machine- and hand-embroidery. It follows a strong tradition of representational embroidery and of landscape painting too, in a typically English watercolour manner. For such work, however, the scale is reasonably big: the piece is 5 × 4ft (1.5 × 1.2m) in a semi-circular frame.

The season of preparatory work from June to August proved exhilarating. There was no embroidery attempted, just drawing, painting and photography in the Derbyshire countryside where Kate painted skies and fields with their shadows and tracks. In the studio more paperwork and making up panoramic collages with the photographic prints followed. In many respects the embroidery itself was a backward step from all of this, as it was clear that in the time available it would not have been possible to experiment with some of the 'painterly' discoveries in the parallel areas of stitchery.

The semi-circular composition presents the awareness of an enormous vision of space – around, above and ahead; the richly embroidered foreground of grasses and flowers indicates movement and vitality which is echoed in the rough hand-stitching in the sky.

The fabric is unbleached cotton canvas. The painting was done with heat-fixed fabric paints in weak dilutions washed on in a watercolour technique. Machine-embroidery over this colour was produced on the Singer 'Irish' industrial machine. This machine stitches freely, swinging up to ½in (12mm) wide. Thread matching the colour is very difficult because a palette of threads is needed to match accurately the many colour mixes in the original painting. This range is established over many pieces of work and extended regularly. Kate finds the hand-embroidery a delightful 'rest' after the activity of the machine work. This employs a simple vocabulary of stitches: Cretan, Roman, Rumanian couching, herringbone, satin, and so forth, using single strands and fine silk threads.

Kate Wells was born in Sheffield. She completed a BA(Hons) in embroidery at Loughborough College of Art and Design in 1976 and an MA (in textiles) at Manchester Polytechnic in 1977. She has been a member of the '62 Group since 1978, exhibiting widely with them both in the United Kingdom and Japan and has lectured and taught in Australia at the invitation of the Creative Embroidery Association of New South Wales. Her work is included in the collection of the Museum of Modern Art in Kyoto, Japan.

Untitled

BEATRICE WILLIAMS

Beatrice Williams claims that her current work has developed out of an interest in the craft traditions of Asia, Central and South America and Africa, but strangely, she makes no mention of the rich cultures that have come together in her own person. Her mother is Welsh and her father is a Guayanese anthropologist, who also writes and paints. Clearly, such a combination might be said to have programmed her to develop an interest in such things as Caucasian animal trappings, Sumac saddle-bags and those decorative disciplines which she acknowledges as influences on her work.

She has lived apart from her father since the age of seven, but visits to him have taken her to such places as the Sudan and West Africa and clearly the colours and forms encountered in those countries have left their imprint on her mental screen.

The untitled piece illustrated here was originally planned to a larger scale, but her final decision was to opt for three rather than five straps. She has evolved a way of working which involves 'cutting through several layers to display a rainbow of multi-coloured edges'. She uses a light-weight Indian cotton for couching and areas of appliqué. Her ambition is to bring to embroidery a more innovative and varied quality.

Beatrice Williams gained a BA(Hons) in textiles at Trent Polytechnic in 1981. Since leaving college she has lectured variously at Loughborough College of Art and Design, Trent Polytechnic, Chesterfield College of Technology and Arts and given various workshops and demonstrations in the East Midlands area where she lives. She was artist in residence for Industry Year (1986) in Nottingham and has also been artist in residence at the Moat Community, sponsored by Marks & Spencer and the Crafts Council.

UNTITLED

ANGELA WYMAN

People looking at Angela Wyman's work frequently ask her if she has travelled in the Middle East or North Africa. Many of the images she employs suggest a knowledge of these places, but her acquaintance with foreign architecture has, so far, been limited to research carried out for a thesis on African art.

She first became interested in the use of felt when she was in her second year at Loughborough College of Art and Jenny Cowern conducted a two-week tutorial in felt-making there.

Her approach to the construction of a piece is to work first in paper, cutting out shapes and arranging and rearranging the pieces as in a paper collage. She finds felt a useful medium to work with because the surface quality can be altered by cutting and stitching onto the surface.

The marble-like quality of the colour gradation in felt that has been dyed is another aspect that attracts her. She commences with a central image as a focal point and encircles this with borders and repeated images, echoing the central image, but subtly altered by gradations of shape or colour. The surface is then enriched with embroidery and the use of matt and shiny threads felted in to link the background with the applied surface decoration.

St Baldred

KATHLEEN WHYTE, MBE

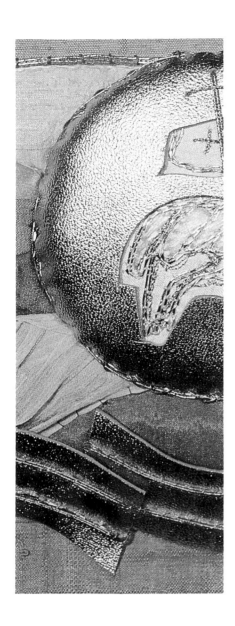

Kathleen Whyte is best known for her ecclesiastical embroidery. 'St Baldred' was commissioned for an agricultural parish, Prestonkirk, Midlothian, near the North Sea. The minister of the parish suggested several subjects for the pulpit-fall: 'The City Set on a Hill', a pastoral scene with a river, a reference to St Baldred, an early Celtic saint who lived on the Bass Rock in the Firth of Forth, and 'The Lamb of God'. He did not suggest that she use all his ideas but Kathleen found that she could incorporate all of them.

She prepared three designs, all based on a cross formation. The component pieces of the design were prepared separately and built up. A certain amount of padding was used to emphasise important features. For example, 'The City Set on a Hill' is made of gold kid pierced in a design suggested by a photograph of Jerusalem and padded with coloured insets. 'The Lamb of God' medallion was made completely, the lamb being embroidered in silver on pure white silk and set into the padded oval. The landscape was also completed and induced to curve forwards, again with padding, to suggest an enveloping feeling with the river bounding the foot. St Baldred is mentioned by name in gold lettering and suggested by a rudimentary Bass Rock at the top of the design.

Since she completed her diploma in art and design with distinction at Gray's School of Art, Aberdeen, in 1932, Kathleen Whyte has taught at various schools in Aberdeen, has been an embroidery teacher at evening classes, served as senior assistant in embroidery and weaving at Glasgow College of Art, organised the first exhibition of the GSA Embroidery Group, been a founder member of five Scottish societies, been guest lecturer to the Chicago Textile Guild, conducted lecture tours in Canada and served on educational panels and boards in England and Scotland. Her book *Design in Embroidery* has run to a second edition and been published in the USA and Holland. She was awarded an MBE in 1969 for services to art education in Scotland.

Kathleen has work included in the collections of the Victoria and Albert Museum, London, The Royal Scottish Museum, the Glasgow Art Gallery, the Scotch Whisky Association, London, and the National Gallery of Victoria in New South Wales.

INDEX